Also by the Authors

By Quin Sherrer

Miracles Happen When You Pray

* * * * *

By Quin Sherrer and Ruthanne Garlock

How to Forgive Your Children
How to Pray for Your Family and Friends
A Woman's Guide to Spiritual Warfare
The Spiritual Warrior's Prayer Guide
A Woman's Guide to Breaking Bondages
A Woman's Guide to Spirit-Filled Living
A Woman's Guide to Getting Through Tough Times
Prayers Women Pray

* * * * *

By Quin Sherrer and Laura Watson

A Christian Woman's Guide to Hospitality

* * * * *

By Ruthanne Garlock

Before We Kill and Eat You
Fire in His Bones
The Christian in Complete Armour, Volumes 1-3
(Senior editor for abridged edition of the
Puritan classic by William G........ll)

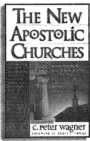
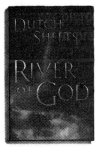

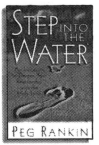

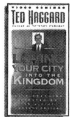

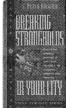

praise for

———— 🐝 ————

How to Pray for Your Children

How to Pray for Your Children is written primarily to mothers,
but fathers also face the challenge of praying for their children
at all stages of their lives. Men will find here a wealth of ideas
and inspiration for fulfilling their godly role as a father.

Dutch Sheets
AUTHOR OF *INTERCESSORY PRAYER*
PASTOR, SPRINGS HARVEST FELLOWSHIP
COLORADO SPRINGS, COLORADO

How to Pray for Your Children is the rich result of Quin Sherrer
speaking to and praying for women all over the world. I couldn't put
it down! I learned so much about how to enrich my prayers for my
children and grandchildren. The portion on praying for your children's
spouses reminded me of the old saying: "They are daughters-in-*love*
and sons-in-*love*. *Love* is when you want to; *law* is when you have to.

Carolyn Sundseth
RELIGIOUS LIAISON TO THE REAGAN WHITE HOUSE
SIERRA VISTA, ARIZONA

This book is destined to make Satan's Most Hated Book list in 1998.
Real-life situations involving every possible agony a parent or grand-
parent can face is found here, but so is the answer—detailed, sustained
prayer! *How to Pray for Your Children* is required reading for parents
who've given up hope or are about to. It's also perfect for expectant
parents. Quin Sherrer and Ruthanne Garlock give us the bottom line:
If you're going to love your children, no matter what they do, you
have to forgive them." Easy? Absolutely not! Possible? *Absolutely.*

Marion Bond West
AUTHOR AND INSPIRATIONAL SPEAKER
CONTRIBUTING EDITOR, *GUIDEPOSTS*
WATKINSVILLE, GEORGIA

How to Pray for Your Children

Quin Sherrer
with
Ruthanne Garlock

Regal

A Division of Gospel Light
Ventura, California, U.S.A.

Published by Regal Books
A Division of Gospel Light
Ventura, California, U.S.A.
Printed in U.S.A.

Regal Books is a ministry of Gospel Light, an evangelical Christian publisher dedicated to serving the local church. We believe God's vision for Gospel Light is to provide church leaders with biblical, user-friendly materials that will help them evangelize, disciple and minister to children, youth and families.

It is our prayer that this Regal book will help you discover biblical truth for your own life and help you meet the needs of others. May God richly bless you.

For a free catalog of resources from Regal Books, Renew or Gospel Light please contact your Christian supplier or call 1-800-4-GOSPEL.

Revised and expanded edition. *How to Pray for Your Children* was originally published by Women's Aglow Fellowship International in 1985.

Cover Design by Barbara LeVan Fisher • Interior Design by Britt Rocchio
Edited by David Webb

Library of Congress Cataloging-in-Publication Data
Sherrer, Quin.
    How to pray for your children / Quin Sherrer with Ruthanne Garlock.
       p.   cm.
    Includes bibliographical references
    ISBN 0-8307-2201-7 (trade paper)
    1. Intercessory prayer—Christianity.   2. Parents—Religious life.
3. Mothers—Religious life.   I. Garlock, ruthanne. I. Title.
    BV210.2.S5145   1998   98-20748
    248.3¹2—dc21   CIP

3 4 5 6 7 8 9 10 11 12 13 14 15 16 17 18 19 20 / 04 03 02 01 00 99

Rights for publishing this book in other languages are contracted by Gospel Literature International (GLINT). GLINT also provides technical help for the adaptation, translation and publishing of Bible study resources and books in scores of languages worldwide. For further information, contact GLINT, P.O. Box 4060, Ontario, CA 91761-1003, U.S.A., or visit their website at glint.org, or contact the publisher.

NOTE: The circumstances of certain events and names of individuals and locations mentioned have been changed to protect the privacy of the persons involved, and to maintain confidentiality.

Contents

Part I
Guidelines for Prayer

Part II

Fighting on the Home Front

Part III

Removing Hindrances to Prayer

Part IV

Establishing a Legacy of Prayer

"Do not be afraid, for I am with you;
    I will bring your children from the east
and gather you from the west.
    I will say to the north, 'Give them up!'
and to the south, 'Do not hold them back.'
    Bring my sons from afar
and my daughters from the ends of the earth
    —everyone who is called by my name,
whom I created for my glory,
    whom I formed and made."

Isaiah 43:5-7

This is what the LORD says:
    "Restrain your voice from weeping
and your eyes from tears, for your work
    will be rewarded," declares the LORD.
"They will return from the land of the enemy.
    So there is hope for your future,"
declares the LORD.
"Your children will return to their own land."

Jeremiah 31:16,17

Foreword

Parents hear many things over the course of a child's lifetime
"Congratulations! It's a boy!"
"Don't worry. He'll grow out of it."
"How could she do that to me?! She's supposed to be my friend."
"Six weeks in a cast and he'll never know it was broken."
"I'm really nervous about my algebra test, Dad."
"Mrs. Johnson? This is the sheriff's department."
"Who gives this woman to be married?"
"Mom, we're having financial problems."
"You're gonna be a grandma!"

Each phone call, each letter, each proclamation evokes a range of thoughts and emotions that only a parent can understand. But no matter what you hear from your child, or about your child, your first response should be—must be—prayer.

Whether you're exultant over his recent scholastic achievement or sharing his grief over the loss of a loved one, whether you're adjusting her veil on her wedding day or anxiously awaiting the results of your unwed daughter's pregnancy test, nothing else can speak to the circumstances or infuse the power of the living God into a life situation like prayer.

Sometimes, your child's situation is clearly out of your hands. Some very funny books, films and television shows have been written about the helplessness we often feel as mothers and fathers. Just as many tragic stories have been told on this theme. Let's face it, sometimes what a child needs, a parent can't provide. Perhaps you, too, have thought, *How can I help my child through this difficulty? Where does it say anything about* this *in the Bible? How can I forgive my son for what he's done?* It's enough to bring you to your knees!

At times like these, openly confess your helplessness before God and lay hold of the one and only effective, practical parenting resource—the one abiding certainty in an unpredictable world—prayer. When you give your child over to God in prayer, the situation is never out of His hands.

Your heavenly Father, the almighty God, will always be there at your child's side. He's available anytime and in every circumstance. It is your right through Christ to approach Him with boldness. As a believer and as a parent, you are *called* to ask of Him, and He has committed to give you as much as you and your child need according to His perfect will.

How to Pray for Your Children shows you how to take hold of this promise and privilege on behalf of your family.

With humor and tenderness, veteran parent and prayer warrior Quin Sherrer has undertaken to equip you for the adventure of working in partnership with the living God. She will guide you to the places in God's Word where you will find answers, peace and wisdom. Hundreds of Scriptures and biblical truths are illustrated with heartrending tales of pain and alienation and, more often than not, heartwarming stories of release and reconciliation in answer to prayer.

We hold our children near to our hearts, giving of ourselves and our love freely and deeply. And so they have the ability to hurt us profoundly. In this book, Quin Sherrer deals honestly and frankly with some very real, very difficult circumstances involving conflict between parents and their children. Not all have yet been fully resolved; nevertheless, these pages are filled with a sense of impending victory—because each of these situations has been released to the Lord in prayer.

Your child is a gift from your Father, a tangible expression of God's love for you. Read this book now and willingly, lovingly give your son or daughter back to God Surrender your hopes and dreams for this child to the One whose children will be mighty in the land (see Psalm 112:2). Give up your worries and plans for provision to the One who knows the number of hairs on the head of each of His children (see Matthew 10:30).

The number of hairs on a child's head is always changing. To know the exact number at any time, God must get very close to them and place His very hand on the heads of our sons and daughters. Let this book be an encouraging reminder of the constant presence of God's hand on the life of your child.

Come now as a disciple of Christ, asking, "Lord, teach us to pray" (Luke 11:1). Then persevere in prayer, dear parent. One day, perhaps, you will hear those wonderful words: "Mom, Dad, thank you. I knew you were praying for me!"

Tim and Beverly La Haye

Acknowledgments

I wish to acknowledge and thank some special pastors who patiently taught me about praying and forgiving: Peter Lord, Forrest Mobley, Dutch Sheets and the late Jamie Buckingham.

Thanks to my three children who have taught me most how to pray and how to forgive—by forgiving me and continuing to be my prayer warriors: Quinett Rae, Keith Alan and Sherry Ruth. And, of course, I am grateful for the patient encouragement of my husband and prayer partner, LeRoy.

Special thanks to Ruthanne Garlock and her husband, John, who have labored with me on eight other book projects. Ruthanne was not only my cowriter on this book, working tirelessly to meet deadlines, but she has stood with me in prayer for my children over the years. From her I have learned much about tenacious prayer.

Thanks also to Fran Ewing, my prayer partner and sounding board; to Gwen Ellis and Carol Greenwood for their original editorial expertise; and to Beth Alves for her years of prayer support.

I greatly appreciate the Reverend Peter Lord of Park Avenue Baptist Church in Titusville, Florida, for giving me permission to use portions of the material from *Learning How to Pray for Our Children*, which I wrote for Agape Ministries while in his church. I also thank those parents who allowed me to share their pains and victories in praying for their children.

To all of you, my sincere gratitude and appreciation.

—*Quin Sherrer*

Introduction

This volume incorporates material from two books I wrote for Aglow International, *How to Pray for Your Children* and *How to Forgive Your Children*.

When I first began writing and teaching on this subject some years ago my husband, LeRoy, and I had just seen our three children return from the land of the enemy—after five long years of intense prayer!

Our children had been in church with us since infants. But they were already in elementary school when LeRoy and I made an all-out commitment to Jesus as our Lord. As renewal swept America in the early 1970s and we attended some of these meetings, God touched our hearts. We invited Him to help us establish a truly Christian home, though we had been teachers and officers in our denominational church for years.

We started family devotional times around our kitchen table, instituted Bible-memorization plans, encouraged our children to keep prayer journals and taught them to pray aloud, even as we were learning. I remember clearly the time each one stood publicly in a church and invited Jesus into his or her heart.

Then came peer pressure, some rebellious years, days away at college when we really didn't know what was happening. This only drove us to prayer.

When we began our prayer venture, there was little written to help us pray for our children. I spent hours digging through the Bible to find God's promises for us and our family. I asked the Holy Spirit to teach us. I listened to pastors, leaders and godly women as they talked to God. I even wrote down some of their prayers. I was after something big—getting hold of God and seeing my prayers answered, my children set free.

LeRoy and I prayed together daily. We learned what "spiritual warfare" meant, though it was years before we would hear that term. We were forced to acknowledge that our enemy—God's enemy, Satan—was determined to keep our children in his camp. But we had God's promises, and we stood on them.

After our five-year prayer battle, our children came back to God, each one in his or her own miraculous way. But that didn't mean we could let down our guard. No, there were still many needs to cover in prayer for them. Financial goals and struggles, health challenges, prayers for their mates and friends, career changes. And, of course, the godly wisdom they need now to raise their own children.

In the years since the first edition of this book was published, I have criss-crossed our nation. I've also gone to more than a dozen others, praying and encouraging mothers to stand in the prayer gap for their families.

Christian parents are hurting for their children today. They are weeping for kids who have run away from home, who are pregnant but not married, who are involved in drugs, sex or occult activities, or struggling with mental illness. I've held mothers in my arms as we wept before the Lord for our children. I know how hearts are breaking.

Mothers, take heart. No matter how hopeless—no matter how impossible your situation seems—God has the answer. He wants to woo our lost, damaged children back to Himself. To do this, He needs us to be faithful in prayer. And we need His wisdom and strength to stand in the gap for our children.

I hope what I have learned on my prayer journey—and the experiences of many other parents who have shared their stories in this book—will challenge, inspire and encourage you. Don't give up. Keep on praying.

—Quin Sherrer

PART I

Guidelines for Prayer

Chapter One

Giving Your Children to God

[Hannah] brought the boy to Eli, and she said to him...
"I prayed for this child, and the Lord has granted me
what I asked of him. So now I give him to the Lord.
For his whole life he will be given over to the Lord."
And he worshiped the Lord there.

1 SAMUEL 1: 25,27,28

"How do you do it? How do you have the stamina to keep going out into that surf?" a tourist asked Keith, my college-age son, one muggy summer morning. She had just watched him pull a fourth swimmer in distress from the Gulf's riptide.

Keith caught his breath as he lay exhausted on the beach beside his lifeguard station, then squinted through the sun to look her in the eye. "Lady, I know I have someone praying for me almost constantly—my mom."

I'm sorry to admit he couldn't always have said that because for years I was a crisis pray-er. When my children got sick, I tried to bargain with God, promising Him all sorts of things if He would only honor my prayer. The rest of the time I uttered only general "bless us" prayers.

Somewhere along the way, I came to realize that if God gave

me three children to rear, it was my responsibility—no, my privilege—to come to Him often on their behalf. But I honestly didn't know how. Surely there was a deeper dimension to prayer than I had experienced.

Thus began my pilgrimage of searching the Bible and listening to others pray. Everywhere I went, I asked mothers, "How do you pray for your children?"

In the ensuing years I've discovered some basic "how-to's" which have helped me, and may help you, too. I start my prayer time with what I call my Three W's. I *worship* the Lord, then *wait* silently asking Him to give me His *Word* to pray for the current situation. Sometimes I use a fourth W— *warfare*—to stand against the enemy's tactics, using the Word of God as my weapon. Always, though, I invite the Holy Spirit to show me how to pray so my prayers are aligned with God's will.

Prayer Helps

Since the Bible encourages us to "enter his gates with thanksgiving and His courts with praise" (Psalm 100:4), I like to begin my prayer time by praising God for who He is and what He does. (See the Appendix for a list of how I use the alphabet to trigger my worship time.)

Prayer also includes asking God's forgiveness—both for sins I remember, as well as those I don't recall. Sometimes I must ask the Holy Spirit to reveal my sins of word, thought, deed, omission or commission. Then I actually say aloud, "Lord, I am truly sorry. Thank you for forgiving me of that."

For me this is a necessary step. I want the line of communication with God completely clear before I begin to petition or intercede for others. I want no unforgiveness, unbelief or unconfessed sin to block my prayers.

Setting formulas for prayer is not always helpful. I'm sharing prayer steps that work for me. You will have others that you have found profitable, too.

1. Be Specific

The blind man told Jesus, "I want to see."

I remember sitting in a Bible school cafeteria listening to the discussion among my son and four of his friends—all single, in their late twenties. They were soon to graduate, and all five wanted to go into missions. But they had no clue as to which country or field they would go, let alone where they'd get the money to go.

I spoke up. "Guys, listening to your conversations, I think your needs can be boiled down to three M's. I'm going to pray for guidance to your particular *mission* field, for *money* to go and a *mate* to love and help you."

"Yeah!" they shouted in unison.

What a great day when Eugene, born in the Philippines but raised in Miami, called me from the land of his birth a year

I hung in there, praying with persistence.
I cried. I fasted. I clung to every promise
God had given me. Today my son
is a mighty man of God.

later. "I found her, Mama Quin," he said excitedly. "Her name is Ruth. We're getting married! You can stop praying for me to find my mate, but keep praying for the money and the right mission station so we can stay here and lead others to Jesus." Today he is a pastor in the Philippines and his wife is a talented musician who assists him.

All five of those Bible school students I started to pray for specifically that day have since served the Lord in extensive ministry. Somehow there was always just enough money to provide for their next trip. God not only called me to invest my time in prayer for them, but also to give financially to help keep some of them where God had placed them. I call this "putting feet" to my prayers.

2. Pray Scripture Passages Aloud

Hearing your own voice speak God's Word strengthens your faith. The Bible declares, "Faith comes from hearing the message, and the message is heard through the word of Christ" (Romans 10:17).

As we pray what Scripture says about our children, the power of God's Word drives out anxiety and fear and produces faith in us. A Bible teacher once explained it this way: "The things we say are the things we will eventually believe, and the things we believe are things we will eventually receive."

When my son was in what I called a temporary state of rebellion, I told him often, "Keith, you are a mighty man of God. You are a force of righteousness." He didn't act like it. He didn't talk like it. But I knew what was deep within him. For five long years I hung in there—believing and praying with persistence. In the meantime, I cried. I fasted. I clung to every promise God had given me. I enlisted others to pray, too. Today Keith is a mighty man of God, having just completed seven years with the Youth With A Mission organization.

3. Write Down Your Prayers

Write out your prayers in a notebook, noting the date. Then record when and how the Lord answered each prayer.

It seems clear that written records are important to God. In Psalm 102 we read, "He will respond to the prayer of the destitute; he will not despise their plea. Let this be written for a future generation, that a people not yet created may praise the Lord" (vv. 17,18). And God commanded the prophet Habakkuk to record the vision he had seen so it would be a witness in the end times (see Habakkuk 2:2,3).

When God speaks to us, we may forget what He's said unless we write it down. But when we record God's promises, it builds our faith. And our children and grandchildren will have proof of God's covenant relationship with us.

4. Pray in Accordance with God's Will

Ask God to reveal the things that are on His heart, then pray His desires for your children. Trust the Holy Spirit to drop thoughts or Scriptures into your mind, and include those ideas in your prayer. Sometimes during your regular Bible reading, verses will seem to leap off the page. These also can become a part of your personal prayers.

5. Pray for Your Children's Future

Remember that some prayers will be "waiting prayers." If you pray for your children's future mates or college choices while they're still young, naturally you will have to wait for the answers. Why not begin praying future prayers now?

A wise gardener plants his seeds, then has the good sense not to dig them up every few days to see if a crop is on the way. Likewise, we must be patient as God brings the answers to our "waiting prayers" in His own good time.

Other Profitable Ways to Pray

In addition to these suggestions, I've discovered other exciting, profitable ways to pray. Some have come by trial and error, others by weeping and travailing, still others through reading my Bible. I've also learned there are ways God does *not* want me to pray—for example, bargaining prayers, selfish prayers, unbelieving prayers or prayers of self-pity.

Armed with God's love, parents can be powerful prayer intercessors for their children. It's usually from mothers that children first hear about God and learn their earliest prayers. May we embrace the challenge to pray for our children, grandchildren, nieces and nephews, as well as other children God brings across our paths. It doesn't matter how old these children are; God loves them and wants none of them to perish.

My own son's acknowledgment of my prayers the summer he was a lifeguard taught me what a privilege it is to pray for our youngsters.

Praying for the Unborn

Actually, it's a good idea to begin praying for our children even before they are born. Scripture contradicts the popular pro-choice notion that a human embryo is only a meaningless mass of cells (see Psalm 139).

In his book, *The Secret Life of the Unborn Child*, Thomas Verny, M.D., reports that clinical studies show a baby in the womb hears, tastes, feels and learns. What he experiences begins to shape his attitudes and expectations about himself. For example, in tests, unborn babies responded calmly to the gentle music of Mozart but reacted with violent motion to performances of Beethoven and rock music. A baby in the womb, Verny says, learns to recognize his parents' voices, is comforted by soothing tones and is upset, fearful and jumpy when parents quarrel.[1]

One couple, during the wife's pregnancy, made a practice of praying for their unborn baby twice a day while laying hands on the mother's abdomen. The father, a minister, wrote about their experience. "Our prayers were spoken out loud, but were simple. We were not trying to communicate with the child except through our attitudes, but we were communicating with God in the child's presence."[2]

Sometimes they prayed for themselves to be the kind of parents they should be for the child. They deliberately did not pray any preference for the baby's sex, not wanting their child to feel any rejection due to their projections of partiality.

At other times they prayed specifically for the baby: "Fill this child with Your presence and Your life. Let this child be especially beloved by You. Watch over Your own child. Fill it with health and happiness and the great desire to be born, a great love for life, an excitement for things spiritual."[3]

One father who prayed over two of his children before their births said, "I'm convinced that we could change our entire nation by simply praying for our unborn and newly born children. It doesn't take special training, only love."

Dedicating Our Children to God

Once while attending a friend's wedding, I was surprised when the pastor paused midway in the wedding ceremony he was conducting for his son. Looking out across the sanctuary, he said, "My friends, I have something I want to share with you. This afternoon before the wedding, my wife and I brought all our children down to the church altar. As they knelt here, we literally gave all five back to God.

"Since our first child is now leaving home, we told the Lord, 'We realize we are only caretakers of these children. We dedicate them once and for all to You.'" I squirmed in my seat. I'd never heard anything like this before, certainly not at a wedding.

"God says in His Word," the pastor continued, "that children are a heritage from Him. I look on ours as gifts entrusted to us for a while."

For several days I couldn't shake what he had said about dedicating his children to God. One morning during my Bible reading, a passage seemed to leap from the page into my heart. It was Hannah's "surrender prayer" to God for her little boy Samuel.

I asked the Lord to give me this child, and he has given me my request. Now I am giving him to the Lord, and he will belong to the Lord his whole life (1 Samuel 1:27,28, NLT).

"Now I am giving him to the Lord...." It rang over and over and over in my mind. I stopped reading, repeated the prayer as my own, and inserted the names of our three children. I thought, *My children are now in junior high, not small like Samuel, but I have today given them back to God.*

Little did I know what a test I'd go through just a few years later when we thought our son was missing at sea. As we gazed across the black, white-capped waves late that summer evening, my husband grabbed my arm and prayed, "God, You know we've dedicated Keith to You. He was baptized in this

Dedicating our children means we will not only depend on the Lord to help us raise them, but that we will accept those children just as God made them.

very gulf at his own request two years ago. Now we commit him totally to You—dead or alive."

My heart pleaded, *Oh Jesus, don't let him be dead. Please find him for us.*

As I walked the beach and prayed, I finally came to a point where I could surrender him unconditionally to his Creator. But, oh, how relieved and thankful I was when he was found safe!

A Mother's Act of Surrender

Becky, a South Dakota mother of seven, wrote to me about her "surrender" experience. "A little more than a year after I had been born again, my husband and I faced a crucial problem with the increasing misbehavior and disobedience of our 14-year-old son," she wrote. "We talked to him, reasoned with him, and punished him, but with little visible effect. His mind was like solid concrete.

"One evening as I was preparing for bed, I sat down on the edge of the bathtub and said, 'God, there is nothing more my husband and I know to do for this child. I give him over to You—completely.'"

Becky calls it "total release." Within three weeks the impossible situation her son had gotten himself into was resolved.

"Undoubtedly, God moved on our behalf," she wrote. "This child was one of the first to ask Jesus to be his Savior. In fact, within six months my entire family, including my husband, seven children, two of their spouses, and one fiancée all were saved. It was not my elaborate prayers. But it was God's Word fulfilled in the life of a believer: 'The prayer of a righteous man [or woman] is powerful and effective' (James 5:16)."

Dedicating our children to God doesn't guarantee that within a matter of months we'll see answers to prayer as Becky did—although it can happen. But such an act of surrender does carry with it great responsibility. It means we'll not only depend on the Lord to help us raise them, but we will also accept those children just as God made them.

My former pastor's wife, Johnnie Lord, taught me much about prayer. When her oldest son, Richard, and a friend drove off from Florida heading for California in an old car with their surfboards, Johnnie admits her imagination went wild. She'd heard all about evil things happening to surfers in those early days of the drug scene.

She kept remembering how she had given Richard to the Lord even before he was born. But now as she battled her fears, she prayed. The Father seemed to say to her, "Johnnie, if I do all *you* want Me to do for Richard, I'll never be able to do what *I* want to do for him."

She writes:

Somehow God was letting me know that from now on things were going to be different. I saw that as our children entered new stages of life our 'giving them to the Lord' had to be extended to include that stage, too....Not without apprehension, I hesitantly but deliberately went around Richard's life and clipped each string, releasing him in a brand-new way to our heavenly Father, so He could work as He needed to accomplish His plan. When the transaction was completed, God's wonderful peace began to move into my heart.[4]

Accept Them, Love Them

I've met some mothers—even Christians—who harbor deep resentments toward their children. One baby disrupted his mother's promising professional career. Another child brought his mother such heartache that she inwardly hated him. "I wish I'd never had him," she cried. I prayed with these women and asked God to enable them to forgive their children so their relationships with them could be healed.

Jesus tells us that if we want our prayers answered, we must forgive: "When you stand praying, if you hold anything against anyone, forgive him, so that your Father in heaven may forgive you your sins" (Mark 11:25).

It's never too late to honestly ask God to forgive your resentment, lack of acceptance, or failure to love a child. He never asks you to do something without giving you the power to do it. So you can also ask Him to give you His love for these children

Don't Give Up Praying

We learn to pray for our children by (1) giving them back to God, (2) forgiving them and (3) loving them unconditionally.

If you are having a hard time liking them, let alone loving them, you might try paraphrasing Romans 5:5 like this: "God, pour out Your love in my heart by the Holy Spirit so I can love with Your love."

At a time when my children were in college and not exactly serving God, I had a dream that was bigger than life. I saw all three of them sitting at the feet of Jesus in a big, open meadow—talking, laughing and listening to Him. I watched from afar as Jesus wrapped an arm around all three in a group hug. There was such a close, personal relationship flowing between them.

I saw myself back away from the scene as I whispered, "Jesus, I leave them in Your care." It was so real that I later said it aloud again, "Jesus, I leave my children in your care."

Did that mean I stopped praying for them? Never. It meant I had moved to a new level of trust in His ability to do with them and for them what I couldn't.

I've lived long enough to see that dream come to pass, as today all three of them have a close, personal relationship with their Lord. After college, when they had each returned to their Christian roots, they attended Bible school. Among the three of them, they have since traveled to four continents doing missions work.

Godly Goals

In addition to specifically dedicating your children to the Lord, here are some godly goals you can begin to pray for them. Add others of your own as you find them in the Scriptures.

1. That Jesus Christ be formed in our children (see Galatians 4:19).
2. That our children—the seed of the righteous—will be delivered from the evil one (see Proverbs 11:21, *KJV*; Matthew 6:13).
3. That our children will be taught by the Lord and their peace will be great (see Isaiah 54:13).
4. That they will learn to discern good from evil and have a good conscience toward God (see Hebrews 5:14; 1 Peter 3:21).
5. That God's laws will be in their minds and on their hearts (see Hebrews 8:10).
6. That they will choose companions who are wise—not

fools, nor sexually immoral, nor drunkards, nor idolaters, nor slanderers, nor swindlers (see Proverbs 13:20; 1 Corinthians 5:11).

7. That they will remain sexually pure and keep themselves only for their spouses, asking God for His grace to keep such a commitment (see Ephesians 5:3,31-33).

8. That they will honor their parents (see Ephesians 6:1-3).

Notes

1. Thomas R. Verny, *The Secret Life of the Unborn Child* (New York: Summit Books, 1981), pp. 19, 20.
2. Francis MacNutt, "Prayers for the Unborn," *Charisma* (November 1983), p. 28.
3. Ibid.
4. Peter Lord, *Keeping the Doors Open* (Grand Rapids: Chosen Books, Fleming H. Revell Company, 1992), pp. 172, 173.

Chapter Two

Keeping a Prayer Journal

*"When you pray, go into your room, close the door and
pray to your Father, who is unseen. Then your Father,
who sees what is done in secret, will reward you."*

MATTHEW 6:6

Do you have a secret place where you go to be alone with
God—a special chair, a garden spot, a private nook, a corner
desk?

The Gospels frequently tell us Jesus went into solitude for
prayer. "He went up on a mountainside by himself to pray"
(Matthew 14:23). Eleven times, Luke mentions Jesus praying.
We, too, need time alone in the Father's presence before we
can be open channels of intercession for our children. Solitude
and quiet will help us pray more effectively.

Knowing God's will is a key to effective prayer. John wrote,
"This is the confidence we have in approaching God: that if we
ask anything according to his will, he hears us. And if we know
that he hears us—whatever we ask—we know that we have
what we asked of him" (1 John 5:14,15).

How do you know God's will? By reading and meditating on
His Word. In it the Lord says, for example, that it is not the
Father's will "that any...should be lost" (Matthew 18:14). So you

can pray in faith for your children to become believers, knowing this is in line with God's perfect will.

Believe He Hears and Answers Our Prayers

Jesus says, "Whatever you ask for in prayer, believe that you have received it, and it will be yours" (Mark 11:24). He also assures us, "My Father will give you whatever you ask in my name" (John 16:23).

Now you can enter triumphantly into your prayer time with Him. I am more convinced than ever of the need to set aside a specific time each day to be with the Lord. I started with just 15 minutes, expanded it to 30, and before long wanted to lengthen it even further.

As active wives, mothers and grandmothers, we sometimes complain we don't have time to pray. We send up "minute prayers" like spiritual arrows while we work at our office desks, iron clothes, make beds, drive carpools or sit in waiting rooms. These prayers are commendable, but God wants quality time with us each day, too.

Whatever time you set aside for Him—morning, noon or evening—it helps to have a few tools on hand: notebook, pen, Bible. Then you're able to record your prayers and God's answers. No "quiet time" is complete until you have not only talked to Him, but also listened to hear our Father's voice. Since we are all different, no two of us will use the same techniques in our personal devotional times.

Prayer has no set pattern, but I have found some practical ways to enrich my private talks with God. Perhaps these will help you, too.

Practical Helps

For nearly 25 years now I've kept personal prayer journals, which I fill with requests, words of praise, reports of answered prayers and specific lessons I'm learning through prayer or Bible reading.

At the beginning of each new year, I get an inexpensive notebook that is divided into five sections. On the first page I paste a picture of our entire family. Underneath our picture I write a paraphrase of a Scripture I prayed daily for our family for years:

> That the God of our Lord Jesus Christ, the glorious Father, may give [us] the Spirit of wisdom and revelation, so that [we] may know him better (Ephesians 1:17).

In the first section of my notebook, I glue a picture of LeRoy and myself and write out our prayer Scriptures. The next three sections contain pictures and prayer requests for our three children and their families. The last section is reserved for others outside our family. Here I place names (and a few pictures) of young people I pray for in the mission field, my children's friends, relatives and some government officials.

In the section for an individual family member, I write Scripture prayers as well as practical prayers I'm praying for that child daily. I often record the date beside specific requests. Later I add the day and the way God answered. This has taught me much about God's perfect timing.

Once I was praying for a daughter away from home who needed a new apartment with lots of storage space. I brought that before the Lord and daily thanked Him that He would provide her with plenty of closets. When He did, I wrote, "Thank You, Lord," and scratched that petition.

This type of prayer action always boosts my faith. I am not a slave to this notebook or method. It's just a helpful vehicle along with my Bible to use for my daily appointment with the Lord.

During my private time, God sometimes speaks to me through my Bible reading. Once in the midst of a personal trial with one of our youngsters, I read about the disciples calling out for Jesus' help as their boat was lashed by a raging storm. "Where is your faith?" He asked them.

Yes, I thought, where was their faith? Jesus had told them to get into the boat and they'd go over to the other side of the lake. His word was trustworthy, wasn't it? Was He not along with them? Why were they worried?

Special moments await you in your secret times of prayer!

Then the Lord spoke to my spirit: "Where is your faith? Haven't I promised you that all your children will be taught of the Lord? Haven't I said I'd bring them back from the land of the enemy? Don't you trust Me with the plans I have for them? I will give them a future and not calamity."

How my heart was pierced!

Actually, those were verses that had lain dormant in my heart for a long time, and I needed them brought back to my memory. Of course, the Lord had promised. And, in a sense, He's always "in my boat," despite my turbulent storms.

One reason I like to quote Scripture verses aloud as prayers is because God has promised that His Word will not return empty or void. It will accomplish what He intends (see Isaiah 55:11). Speaking His Word aloud builds my faith in the One who works all things to my good and the good of my children, too.

Recording God's Directions

You may want to get a notebook and write down any impressions the Lord gives you during your time with Him. If you've never done it before, you'll find it exciting.

A mother I know tried this idea with her prayers for her rebellious teenage daughter, Sue. She asked God to show her how to love Sue and to teach the girl how to respond to that love.

Whenever little thoughts came to her that were related to Sue, she wrote them down in a notebook, such as, "Don't go grocery shopping until Sue can go with you. Don't buy Sue's clothes until she can help you select them. Let Sue help you cook supper. Choose some of her favorite dishes."

These may sound insignificant, but as this mother began to do them, she saw a softening in her daughter. Gradually, Sue's attitude changed and so did her appearance. Her body slimmed down and her personality blossomed. It was not an overnight miracle by any means but a slow metamorphosis.

The mother had learned a significant lesson. She told me that God didn't take away Sue's self-will; He just converted it into what He put it there for in the first place. Sue soon turned her life over to the Lord completely and became strong in her convictions. In fact, she was no longer rebellious or easily led astray by her peers. Today Sue is happily married to a fine Christian and can hardly remember that troubled period in her life.

Oh, what special moments await you in your secret times of prayer! How your heavenly Father longs to hear your prayers for your children.

Let me share two prayers of a pastor's wife:

"Lord, I want Your love to be free today to flow through me, so fill my mind with ways to reach out in love to my family members, _____ (name them)."

"God, what do You want me to trust You for today in the lives of my children?" (Write down your impressions as they come.)

Special Journal Entries
Here are some entries from my prayer journal over the years:

Heal Her Broken Heart
Lord, our daughter's heart is broken. Please comfort her. It was her first touch of love, and

now he's dumped her for another girl. Her pride is wounded. She feels rejected, worth nothing. Oh, Lord, may she realize how much You love her and we love her. Heal her hurts. Bring other Christian friends into her life who can help fill the void left after losing her special friend. Help her get her priorities in order and realize her real purpose in life should be to love and please You. Thank You for Your everlasting arms around our daughter—Your daughter.

Help with Exam
Lord, he has an important exam today. He's studied long and hard. Yet he's anxious, with butterflies inside. Quiet his spirit. Bring to his mind all the things he's studied and stored away for this moment. Help him to do his best. Thank You, Lord.

Help Her Accept Herself
Lord, our daughter is almost two heads taller than the other girls in her class. She feels like a giant. Show her You made her just like she is for a purpose. You know what You have in store for her, not only in her physical makeup but with the abilities You have given her. She's struggling hard right now to find her true identity. Please help her see she is special and unique, just as each of Your children is.

Help Me Be an Encourager
Lord, he's not doing as well in school as I'd like. Help me accept his pace. Though I'd like better grades, keep me from pushing him beyond his capacity. Show me how to encourage him, right where he is.

Let Him Forgive Me

Today I lost my cool and said some cutting things I wish I could take back. I hurt my son with words. As I ask him to forgive me, restore our relationship, Lord. Help me know when to correct and when to keep silent. Lord, I want to manifest the fruits of Your Spirit in my life— love, joy, peace, patience, kindness, goodness, faithfulness, gentleness and self-control.

Draw Her Back

God, I watch so helplessly as our teenager drifts away from You, though we gave this child to You at birth. I remember when I was a teen—I, too, questioned and rebelled. But in Your loving time, You drew me back—stronger, firmer, more sure than ever of the reality of the risen Lord, my Savior. Do so with our child. O God, do so again. Thank You that You do answer mothers' prayers.

Marriage Decision

Lord, make it clear to him if she's the one to be his helpmate. Help them both grow up in You, Lord. Cut off their rough edges so they'll be ready for marriage. If they are to be life partners, thank You. If not, take her away from him without rejection or wounding.

Demonstrate Your Greatness

Today is a big day on the job for her—a day to make a presentation before the bosses. Move in a mighty way on her behalf, Lord. Demonstrate Your greatness in her life that others may see You. Protect her body, mind and spirit and give her Your peace.

Moving Prayers

She's anticipating a job change in a couple of months. O, Lord, lead her to the job of Your choice in the town of Your choice where she can use her education, skills and ability to the best capacity. Continue to release Your flow of creativity in her. Guide her, too, to the right church, right roommates and right apartment complex. I give You thanks in advance, for You are a faithful, loving Father. Thank You that this adult child of mine continues to love and serve You with her gifts.

Accomplish Your Will

Today accomplish Your will in my children's lives, Father. Have mercy on them according to Your lovingkindness.

Two Job Offers

Lord, it hardly seems possible. When we prayed for a new job for him, he got two good offers! Give him wisdom and discernment to make the right choice. Thank You, Lord.

Daughter's Talents

For a daughter who is an interior designer and makes sacred banners for churches, I personalized an Old Testament verse: "Lord, may Quinett be filled with skill to do all kinds of work as a craftsman, designer, embroiderer in blue, purple and scarlet yarn and fine linen, and weaver—as a master craftsman and designer" (see Exodus 35:35).

Son's Specific Talent

For my son, who is a graphic artist, I wrote: "May Keith be filled with the Spirit of God, with skill, ability and knowledge in all kinds of crafts—to make artistic designs and to engage in all kinds of artistic craftsmanship" (see Exodus 35:31-33).

Girlfriend or Future Wife?

Lord, are he and Dana to be good friends, or is this a relationship that will lead to marriage? Show both of them. Don't let them be drawn to each other from a "need" orientation, but may their friendship be holy and of your design, Lord. Give both of them a clear understanding of what their relationship is to be even after they graduate. May Your will be done in their lives. I call for Your best—nothing less—in both their lives. Trusting You, Amen.

Praise for Answered Prayer

Last September while I was in church, You showed me in my mind's eye all three of our children with arms uplifted praising You, Lord. I wrote in my journal that I accepted that picture and would stand in faith until it was fulfilled. Today in looking back over my prayer journal, I was reminded again how faithful You are. After only eight months, You've brought all three into a deeper commitment, a closer walk. Indeed, they are singing Your praises with uplifted arms. Oh, thank You, Lord. Thank You, Lord.

Wisdom and Discernment

Lord, give my children wisdom about what they are to look at and listen to. Help them avoid those things that would defile their minds (1 Peter 1:13-16).

Lord, let my children hate this rock music that is so attractive to them now when they are in their teens. May they have a desire to hear music restful for their souls.

Answer:
Some ten years later when I was Christmas shopping with my oldest, she was so repelled by the loud rock music, she said to the store manager, "Will you please turn your music down or off if you want me to stay and shop here."

Inside I was praising God for answered prayer. Soft, soothing music is her choice nowadays.

* * * * *

Lord, in a day—suddenly—You can move. My child needs a miracle. Let her see You have been faithful. Let her be encouraged and excited about what You have in store for her.

My faith is building, Lord, to believe for a sudden answer to my prayer for my child. Today I read again how when the apostle Peter was in jail, You suddenly sent an angel to rescue him. Even at a time when a night prayer meeting was going on for him (see Acts 12:6-12). Lord, I've prayed for this child so long. Turn her situation around. I thank You in advance for doing so, precious Lord.

* * * * *

Lord, You said the angel of the Lord encamps around those who fear You and rescues them (see Psalm 34:7). Rescue my child. How she needs rescuing!

* * * * *

It breaks my heart, Lord, to hear her so discouraged as we talk long distance on the phone. Bring some Christian friends into her life who can be encouragers to her.

* * * * *

Thank You for Your traveling mercies as my children drive back and forth to jobs. Protect them and give them wisdom to drive safely and sanely.

* * * * *

Lord, awaken in her a fresh understanding of Your plan for her life. May she soon walk in the joy Jesus gives which enables one to overcome disappointment and pain, heartache—agony of spirit.

* * * * *

Open new windows of hope, Lord.

* * * * *

Thank You, Lord, for her metamorphosis. Thank You that spring has come in her life. New job. New hope. New joy. Help her in her relationships with her boss and employers. May they appreciate her job skills and not pressure her to overwork. She's so excited. So am I.

Thank You for answered prayer. Together, she and I give You praise! Amen.

Sample Prayer Journal Page

Child's Name _____

Thank You, Lord, that You know the
plans You have for _____
to prosper and not harm him/her,
but to give him/her hope and a
future. I pray that my child will
not stand in the way of sinners
or sit in the seat of mockers. May
my child's delight be in the law
of the Lord as he/she meditates
on it day and night (see Jeremiah
29:11; Psalm 1:1,2).

Place

photo of

child here

Dear Father, may _____ , like Your Son
Jesus, grow in wisdom and stature, and in favor with You
and the people his/her life touches. Give him/her a listening ear to parental instructions. Help him/her to pay
attention that he/she may gain understanding (see Luke
2:52; Proverbs 4:1).

May the Spirit of the Lord rest upon my child,
_____ —the Spirit of wisdom, understand-
ing, counsel, might, knowledge and the reverential and
obedient fear of the Lord (see Isaiah 11:2, *Amp.*). I pray the
eyes of his/her heart may be enlightened in order that
he/she may know You better. I pray that Christ may dwell
in his/her heart through faith and that _____ will
be rooted and established in love (see Ephesians 1:17; 3:17).

Chapter Three

Battling with Persistence

"So I say to you: Ask and it will be given to you; seek and you will find; knock and the door will be opened to you. For everyone who asks receives; he who seeks finds; and to him who knocks, the door will be opened."

LUKE 11:9,10

Some years ago a friend of mine discovered her unmarried son was about to become a father. She fasted, prayed, wept and read her Bible for several days. Then God reminded her that years earlier He had promised that her son would be a committed, anointed man of God.

"I still stand on that promise in faith," she told our prayer group. "Someday my son will be an example of God's forgiving and restoring goodness, even though he isn't yet. God will restore."

It has been a years-long battle of prayer for this young man. Yet my friend continues to intercede with persistence, confident she will see victory in her son's life. She realizes this heartache can be a time of learning and training for future usefulness. Her son's resistance to God doesn't sway her, because her faith is rooted in God's promises.

But she is learning the reality of what many parents have learned: We must pay a price to see our children come into His Kingdom. We can't give up praying!

Jesus clearly taught the importance of specific requests and persistence in the parable of a man who kept knocking until his sleepy neighbor roused at midnight to give him three loaves of bread for his unexpected guests. He made a specific request, he was persistent in asking, and he got exactly what he came for.

Jesus concluded the parable by saying we should continue seeking, knocking and asking until our prayer is answered (see Luke 11:5-13). One commentator, Pastor Jack Hayford, offers this insight:

> Jesus teaches persistence in prayer, along with a sense of urgency and boldness. He does not suggest that we must overcome God's reluctance to respond to our requests, but that we must be earnest and wholehearted in prayer. The persistence is necessary for our benefit, not for God's.[1]

It's important that we not give up praying for the following reasons:

- To guard our minds so the enemy cannot harass us regarding prayers not yet answered.
- So we don't become discouraged, but are inwardly strengthened to walk in love. (Remember, as you are praying for family members and the Holy Spirit is working in their lives, the enemy will try to bring strife and division between you.)
- To be alert to the snares the enemy would set for those for whom we are praying.

Persistence Without Visible Evidence

Let's examine the faith and persistent prayer of one of God's key prophets, Elijah. After Israel had suffered a three-and-a-half-year drought, the Lord told Elijah to present himself to King Ahab, and He would send rain.

The prophet confidently told the king, "Go, eat and drink, for there is the sound of a heavy rain" (1 Kings 18:41). Elijah expected rain to come because God had promised it.

Yet when he spoke those words to Ahab, there was absolutely no visible evidence that rain was about to drench the sun-parched land. What did the prophet do? He climbed to the top of Mt. Carmel and crouched down on the ground with his head between his knees. Seven times he sent his servant to look for a sign that rain was coming, but the servant kept returning to say, "There is nothing there" (v. 43).

In the Middle East this was the posture of women when they were giving birth. It's as if Elijah is birthing the answer to his prayer, which he had already declared to Ahab. When the first tiny "sign" appeared, it was a cloud only the size of a man's hand. A pint-sized sign to some eyes, but not to Elijah's. Before long the sky grew black with clouds, and heavy rain poured down.

My pastor, Dutch Sheets, comments on Elijah's fervent prayer in his book, *Intercessory Prayer.* "Please don't miss the implication of this passage," he writes. "Even though it was God's will to bring the rain and it was also God's time for the rain, someone on earth still had to birth it through prayer."[2]

Years ago, I relived this scene in my mind's eye as I stood atop Mt. Carmel in Israel. Looking out over the lush green plains, I remembered Elijah's boldness. How I longed to have the same confidence in God's Word which Elijah exhibited in this test of his faith.

Later I was encouraged to read in James 5:17,18 that Elijah was a person with a nature like ours, not some exalted dignitary. As an ordinary human being, he offered his earnest prayers in faith.

How can we apply the lesson of Elijah's prayer experience to our own?

Sometimes the Lord gives assurance that our children are coming out of their rebellion or their crisis situation, though we don't see any visible evidence. In fact, the circumstances may look worse than ever before. That is the time to believe God, stand on His Word, and thank Him in advance for answered prayer. In the meantime, we pray persistently, sometimes in travail, letting the Holy Spirit in us groan with words that cannot even be expressed (see Romans 8:26).

Labor Before Birth

Intercession is often compared to the birthing process: conception, gestation, labor and, ultimately, delivery. Sadly, many parents give up on intercession too quickly. Someone once said, "Waiting is a greenhouse where doubts flourish." As time passes, parents can be overwhelmed by doubts that things will ever change.

Near the end of my first pregnancy, I'd had heavy labor pains on and off for two days and nights in a rural Florida hospital that was greatly understaffed. On the third morning, a Sunday, I was ready to quit. I packed my bag, waddled out of the hospital, and was standing on the side of the highway when LeRoy and Mother drove up to visit me.

"I'm tired of going through labor," I told LeRoy when he got out of the car. "I've decided I'm not going to have this baby. Take me home."

"Honey, you can't quit now," he said, guiding me back into the hospital. "Go back and labor just a little more," he pleaded. "The baby will come."

My doctor came in and decided to induce labor. I still remember that intense pain! At times, LeRoy and Mom together had to hold me down on the bed. We labored together, pushing, encouraging, fighting for the baby's birth. Six hours later, our eight-and-a-half pound daughter, Quinett, came into the world—bruised, red and crying, but healthy.

An enormous struggle—yes! But what a rich reward we had in the birth of our precious baby! Labor always precedes birth—sometimes long, hard labor. Let's review the stages involved in birthing a child, and compare them to "birthing in the spirit" through prayer:

1. Conception—when your prayer becomes one with God's desire.
2. Gestation—when God enlarges the vision of His plan and you have faith to pray for it.
3. Labor—travailing and believing; only then does birthing take place.

One Mother's Struggle

My friend Audrey learned the spiritual reality of this process in the crisis she went through with her son, Victor. A few days before he was to graduate from high school, he learned he'd failed his Advanced English course and would not be allowed to participate in the graduation ceremony. Three days later he disappeared, leaving this note on the windshield of Audrey's car: "Mother, Dad...I have to get away. Don't worry. Vic."

"This was a complete shock, as Vic had never given me any problem," Audrey told me. "Other members of my family had caused me grief, but I had such high expectations that Vic would serve the Lord with all his heart in whatever career he chose. All I could do was to call on the Lord for help."

After searching frantically for her son, Audrey finally located one of his close friends. "If you hear from Vic, please have him call home," she begged.

That night the phone rang. A weak voice on the other end of the line breathed a terse message: "Mom, I'm all right." Then Vic cut the connection, leaving her no clue as to his whereabouts.

"I had one choice, and I knew it," Audrey shared as she recalled the experience. "If I were to survive emotionally, I had to forgive Vic for the disappointment I felt because he was not graduating, and for his leaving home without so much as a good-bye. I also had to lay down my pride, my hurt and finally my anger. Otherwise I'd be tormented by what he had done to me, and worrying about where he was. So I made the choice: I forgave Vic, releasing all my pent-up feelings as I committed him once again into God's care."

After that came a period of gestation—simply waiting for God to fulfill His promises regarding Victor. Audrey continued to pray tenaciously, but she kept declaring that her son was in God's hands. "Lord, you know where Vic is; I don't. Watch over him. Please see that he has a place to stay, clean sheets and food to eat."

Seeing Things Differently

From that time on, whenever Audrey drove past young men hitchhiking, she prayed for each one. "I knew my boy was probably out there somewhere, too," she explained. "My whole outlook on runaways who thumb rides with strangers changed. To this day I pray for hitchhikers I see on the side of the road."

Three months after Vic's disappearance, Audrey woke up feeling she should contact one of his friends who worked at a downtown music store. She somehow felt her son was back in the area. Finding her son's friend at his job, she pushed a piece of paper into his hand and said, "If you see Vic, please give him this."

The note read: "Vic, I'll come get you on Sunday for lunch. Mom." That evening the friend called to say Vic would be ready at noon on Sunday, and he gave directions to his apartment in a bad section of town.

The following Sunday, after asking her friends to pray she wouldn't cry and fall apart when she saw him, she drove to the apartment. A frail, thin boy wearing a threadbare sweater silently climbed into her car. It had been 94 days since she had seen her son.

"Hello, Vic," she said quietly.

"Hello, Mom. I missed you."

Those words from Vic opened the door for their relation-ship to begin mending. Audrey received him with love and resisted plying him with questions about why he ran away. Back at his mom's table, Vic devoured her fried chicken dinner. For a few minutes, only his teary eyes expressed his gratitude.

"Mom, I want you to know there was
never a night when I didn't have food
and a place to stay with clean sheets."
What a God!

Finally able to speak, he said, "Mom, this is so good. I want you to know there was never a night when I didn't have a place to stay with clean sheets. And I always had food of some kind."

What a God! Audrey's heart ignited with praise to learn her specific prayers were answered. Vic told her he had left North Carolina with only $23 in his pocket, hitchhiking first to New York and then to New Mexico. Overwhelmed by failure when he couldn't graduate, he had chosen to run away rather than face anybody. Now he was back in town, holding down a menial job.

A Long Road to Restoration

After Vic left, Audrey appealed to her husband to allow their son to move back home. "Absolutely not," he replied. "He chose to run away on his own—let him make it on his own." But Audrey again invited Vic for a Sunday lunch, and prayed fervently her husband would soften. After six weeks, he agreed Vic could come home.

With Audrey's encouragement, he earned his high school diploma, then studied at a junior college and, later, at a technical college. Next came a brief marriage that ended in divorce, but this persistent mom kept praying.

Finally, at age 28, Vic committed his life to Christ. A few

years later he married a wonderful Christian girl from Europe. Throughout their wedding ceremony, Audrey kept whispering gratefully, "Thank you. Thank you. Thank you, Lord."

In talking about her victory, Audrey was emphatic about the connection between love and forgiveness. "If you're going to love your children, no matter what they do, you have to forgive them," she said.

"I'd be fooling myself if I didn't admit there were plenty of times I had to forgive Vic after he moved back home. And I was heartbroken when his first marriage failed. It seemed he was in the enemy's territory for a long, long time. I just had to keep on forgiving him and keep on praying—but I'm so glad I did. Thank God for His faithfulness."

Conflict in the Spiritual World

As we travail to see spiritual birth take place in our children's lives, we soon find we're involved in the kind of conflict the apostle Paul wrote about:

> We are not fighting against people made of flesh and blood, but against persons without bodies—the evil rulers of the unseen world, those mighty satanic beings and great evil princes of darkness who rule this world; and against huge numbers of wicked spirits in the spirit world (Ephesians 6:12, *TLB*).

These forces of darkness hinder the truth of the gospel, blinding and deceiving our children (see 2 Corinthians 4:4). Another passage compares the devil to a roaring lion prowling about, looking for someone to devour (see 1 Peter 5:8). Rest assured that our children are among his targets.

An intercessor sometimes stands between God and a person pleading for Him to intervene. At other times, she stands between the enemy and that same person, battling. Our prayer is directed toward God, and our warfare is directed toward the enemy.

Weapons of Warfare

The good news is that Jesus, the Son of God, came to earth to destroy the works of the devil. Jesus defeated Satan at the Cross, and the Father has put all things under His feet. Jesus tells His followers to exercise authority over the power of the enemy until His return (see 1 John 3:8; Ephesians 1:22; Luke 10:18,19).

Following are some of the weapons available to Christians as we pray and battle against the enemy:

The Name of Jesus	Mark 16:17,18; Luke 10:17-19; Philippians 2:9-11
The Blood of Jesus	Colossians 2:14,15; Hebrews 9:12-14
Agreement	Ecclesiastes 4:9,10; Matthew 18:19,20
Binding and Loosing	Matthew 16:19; Mark 3:27
Fasting	Isaiah 58:6; Matthew 6:16-18; Luke 4:2
Praise	2 Chronicles 20:14-22; Psalm 149:6-9
Word and Testimony	Ephesians 6:17; Hebrews 4:12; Revelation 12:11

Although we have not fully understood the relationship between prayer and spiritual warfare, the Holy Spirit can teach us how to pray more effectively and how to do battle spiritually. Our confidence is in Jesus, our Commander, who promises we will see victory!

Paul reminds us, "The weapons we fight with are not the weapons of the world. On the contrary, they have divine power to demolish strongholds" (2 Corinthians 10:4).

Our faith is not in our own ability to pray or to battle; it is in God's assurance that the weapons He provides are strong enough to destroy the enemy's plans. We have the responsibility, through prayer and spiritual warfare, to snatch our children out of Satan's strongholds.

Authority in Jesus' Name

Jesus appointed a group of followers (Luke 10:1-20) and gave them His authority to "overcome all the power of the enemy" through His name (v. 19). The name of Jesus is not simply a magic word. When we are in right relationship with Him, we too have the authority to use His name as a weapon to overpower the works of the evil one.

Paul Billheimer wrote of his own experience with this weapon:

> Many believers have been so tyrannized and dominated by Satan and the prevailing theology of Satan's power and invincibility that, like me, they would never dare to speak directly to him, even in the name of Jesus.
>
> James's exhortation to resist encouraged me to face that roaring lion (see James 4:7). When I mustered enough courage to speak directly to him in the name of Jesus, it was a great surprise to me to discover an immediate sense of deliverance.
>
> Our resistance by itself is not what causes Satan to flee; he flees because of the power of Jesus which is ours through prayer.[3]

Bible teacher Dean Sherman reminds us:

> The authority is complete in man as long as man is in relationship with God through Jesus Christ. With our authority comes the responsibility to use it for God's purposes. If we don't rebuke the devil, he will not be rebuked. If we don't drive him back, he will not leave. It is up to us. Satan knows of our authority, but hopes we will stay ignorant. We must be as convinced of our authority as the devil is.[4]

Jesus' Blood Defeated the Enemy

When Israel was preparing to leave Egypt, Moses instructed each family to sacrifice a lamb on behalf of their household. They sprinkled the blood on their doorposts in order to be spared when the angel of death passed by (see Exodus 12:1-13). Through this miraculous deliverance of the nation, God established the observance of the Passover.

The spilling of many lambs' blood in Egypt was a precursor of the sacrifice of Christ, the Lamb of God, whose blood shed on the Cross defeated Satan. In overcoming this enemy,

For three years her son remained defiant.
Today he is serving the Lord, leading
thousands of young people out of their
rebellion against God.

Scripture tells us that Christ "disarmed the powers and authorities, he made a public spectacle of them, triumphing over them by the cross" (Colossians 2:15).

We can use the blood of Jesus as a weapon by declaring aloud that the work of the Cross destroyed Satan's power. God raised His Son from the dead, exalted Him far above all evil rulers, and placed Satan's emissaries under the feet of Christ (see Ephesians 1:19b-22). We can remind the enemy that the blood of Jesus not only purchased our salvation, it also sealed his total defeat.

Arthur Mathews, author of *Born for Battle,* wrote, "Blessed is that intercessor who knows how to use the power of the blood in spiritual warfare."[5]

One mother I know used this weapon in spiritual warfare when her son went into rebellion. He had served the Lord many years, but rebelled when he fell into bad company. He then moved out of the house, and she didn't know where he was.

A part of her strategy was to go into his room, now empty, and say to the enemy, "My son is covered by the blood of Jesus, and your plan to keep him in your kingdom of darkness will not succeed. I declare that the blood of Jesus defeats your plan, Satan, and he will repent and come back to God!"

For three years her son remained defiant. But today he not only is serving the Lord, he has led many thousands of young people out of their rebellion against God, and trained them to win others to Christ.

Agreement Is Strategic

Effective praying is prayer which is in agreement with God's Word and is led by the Holy Spirit. This is why I emphasize the importance of waiting on God for direction. We fallen human beings easily slip into praying manipulative prayers that serve our own selfish desires. But when we immerse ourselves in God's Word and ask the Lord to show us how to pray in a given situation, He helps us to see our problem from His perspective.

Jesus promised, "If two of you on earth agree about any-thing you ask for, it will be done for you by my Father in heaven. For where two or three come together in my name, there am I with them" (Matthew 18:19,20). When we pray in agreement with God's will, and have a prayer partner agreeing with us, the force of the prayer increases. Also, we greatly strengthen our own faith in this way. The next chapter will explain how to pray in agreement.

Binding the Enemy's Work

We have no power over another person's will. But we do have Jesus' power-of-attorney, so to speak, to bind the evil forces or powers blinding people against receiving the truth. Jesus said what we bind on earth will be bound in heaven, and what we loose on earth will be loosed in heaven (Matthew 16:19).

This principle is illustrated by the case of the mother and grandparents of a runaway girl in Florida. They decided to do spiritual warfare every afternoon on the girl's behalf. "Remember that your spiritual warfare for Cynthia cannot overpower her will," their pastor counseled. "It does, however, bind the power of evil forces blinding her and affecting her will, and releases her to see the truth, then make decisions freely."

Every day they declared aloud, "You evil, deceiving spirits seeking to lead astray and destroy our child, Cynthia, we bind you in the name of Jesus Christ. We are seated together with Christ in spiritual authority, and we tell you to take your hands off Cynthia's life. Release her will, so she may be free to accept Jesus Christ as Savior, Lord and Deliverer." (See 2 Timothy 2:25b,26).

Then they prayed, "Holy Spirit of God, draw our child from the camp of the enemy. Reveal Your love to her. Thank You, Lord, for placing a hedge of protection about her."

After a few weeks of their praying this way, the girl returned home. One of the first things she said to her mother was, "Tell me about Jesus." Today she is walking with Him.

Benefits of Fasting

Fasting—abstaining from food—coupled with prayer can yield several results: direction from God, a closer walk with the Lord, a humbling of self, healing, even answers to prayer. Because of medical conditions, some people cannot give up food completely. Some fast by taking only juices or other liquids. Others give up one meal or more in a day. Some "fast" certain types of food.

We should ask for God's direction when we enter a period of fasting. But it is important to allow God time to speak to us through His Word and as we pray and wait upon Him. In his book, *God's Chosen Fast*, Arthur Wallis states:

We must not think of fasting as a hunger strike designed to force God's hand and get our own way! Prayer, however, is more complex than simply asking a loving father to supply his child's needs. Prayer is warfare. Prayer is wrestling. There are opposing forces. There are spiritual crosscurrents.

The man who prays with fasting is giving heaven notice that he is truly in earnest: that he will not give up nor let God go without the blessing.[6]

Praise Confuses the Enemy

A key weapon at our disposal is praise. Satan's fetters are broken when we verbalize praise to the Most High God and declare His victory (see Psalm 149:6-8). Reading the Psalms makes us aware that we should praise God whatever our circumstances, simply because God is worthy of our praise.

When Paul and Silas were thrown into prison for preaching the gospel, they sang hymns and praised God from their cell—even in the midnight hour. In the night, an earthquake shook the prison and they were freed (see Acts 16:16-26). Imagine the state of confusion in the ranks of the enemy when that prison was demolished! This account underscores the importance of praising God before we see the victory.

Satan hates praise because it focuses our attention on God and declares his own defeat. Use it as a power-packed weapon to demolish strongholds, and to remind the enemy his schemes against our children are null and void because of Christ's victory at the Cross.

Using the Word as a Weapon

I remember my days of walking the floor, battling enemy forces for my children's deliverance. Following Jesus' example of using God's Word as a weapon, I spoke aloud, "It is written..." (Matthew 4:4,7,10).

Then I prayed various Scriptures. "The seed of the righteous shall be delivered....My children shall be taught of the Lord, and great will be their peace....Thank you, Lord, that you will give your angels charge over my child to guard him in all his ways" (see Proverbs 11:21; Isaiah 54:13; Psalm 91:11).

As you prayerfully study God's Word, the Holy Spirit can lead you to the exact Scriptures to pray that are appropriate for your current situation. You can paraphrase the verses and insert your children's names as you build your own personal arsenal of Scripture prayers for your family.

The weapons of warfare God provides for us are effective, if we have the discipline to use them. I remember a time when I was discouraged because some of my prayers for my children weren't yet answered. The Lord sent Paul Billheimer and his wife, Jenny, to have a meal at my table and encourage me. The story he shared with me that night about the power prayers of his own mother appears in one of his books:

My mother used these weapons on me. I was as hostile to God as any sinner. I was fighting with all my might. But the time came when it was easier to lay down my arms of rebellion than to continue my resistance. The pressure exerted upon me by the Holy Spirit became so powerful that I voluntarily sought relief by yielding my rebellious will. The wooing of divine love was so strong that of my own free will I fell into the arms of redeeming grace. I became a willing "captive."[7]

That testimony motivated me to take up my weapons and continue the battle, despite the negative circumstances of the moment. I was reminded of this promise:

But thanks be to God, who always leads us in His triumph in Christ, and manifests through us the sweet aroma of the knowledge of Him in every place (2 Corinthians 2:14, NASB).

How thankful I was to be reminded that if I simply remained faithful in prayer, God would see us through to victory because His Son paid the price to defeat our enemy.

Prayer

Heavenly Father, I come to You on behalf of _____.
I pray that he be delivered from every scheme and snare the devil has used to hold him captive. Let every stronghold of unbelief and vain imagination in his life be pulled down, and brought into captivity to the obedience of Christ (see 2 Corinthians 10:5).

Lord, work in his life so he will realize how he needs You. Show him he must call upon You to be saved. Send laborers across his path to speak into his life and reveal Your truth. Thank You, Lord, that my child is coming out of bondage because of Your mercy. In Jesus' name, Amen.

* * * * *

Thoughts to Ponder:

Sometimes when you are praying and reading the Scriptures, the Lord might highlight one of these as a reason your children have not turned their hearts toward God. If He does, ask Him for a prayer strategy. Of course, these aren't the only reasons people don't choose Jesus:

- Satan has blinded them (see 2 Corinthians 4:4).
- Satan has held them captive to do his will (see 2 Timothy 2:26).
- Worries of this world, deceitfulness of riches and desire for other things choke out the Word of God (see Mark 4:19).

- Unforgiveness. Listed in 2 Corinthians 2:10,11 as a scheme of the devil. Also see Mark 11:25,26.
- Not enough harvesters in the field. Ask the Lord of the harvest to send out workers (see Matthew 9:38).

Notes

1. Jack Hayford's commentary on Luke 11:5-10, *Spirit-Filled Life Bible* (Nashville: Thomas Nelson, 1991), p. 1535.
2. Dutch Sheets, *Intercesssory Prayer* (Ventura, Calif.: Regal Books, 1996), p. 132.
3. Paul E. Billheimer, *Destined to Overcome* (Minneapolis: Bethany House, 1982), pp. 41, 43.
4. Dean Sherman, *Spiritual Warfare for Every Christian* (Seattle: Frontline Communications, 1990), p. 123.
5. Arthur Mathews, *Born for Battle* (Robesonia, Pa.: OMF Books, 1978), p. 63.
6. Arthur Wallis, *God's Chosen Fast* (Fort Washington, Pa.: Christian Literature Crusade, 1968), pp. 41, 42.
7. Paul Billheimer, *Destined for the Throne* (Christian Literature Crusade: Fort Washington, Pa., 1975), pp. 17, 18.

Chapter Four

Finding Strength in Agreement

"Again, I tell you that if two of you on earth agree about anything you ask for, it will be done for you by my Father in heaven. For where two or three come together in my name, there am I with them."
MATTHEW 18:19,20

When we get serious about praying for our children, we soon discover that praying with a prayer partner strengthens our effectiveness and encourages us.

Two of the more than 50 reciprocal commands in the New Testament include these "one anothers": pray for one another and bear one another's burdens.

Not only do we help carry each other's burdens, but we rejoice together over answered prayers. When praying with others we learn we aren't the only parents in the world going through difficulties with our children.

Get a Special Friend to Pray

Every Christian woman needs a special friend who will share her secret problems, needs and concerns without divulging them to anyone but the Lord.

The word "agree" in our opening Scripture is derived from

the Greek word from which we get our word "symphony." It means "to be in accord or in harmony" or "to make one mind." We could translate this verse: "If two of you have harmony in the Spirit concerning anything that you ask, it will be done."

Jesus never did or said anything except what the Heavenly Father told him to do—thus He was always in agreement with Him. Of course we want to be praying in God's will, not making selfish, manipulative demands.

One couple who prayed together daily for their daughters told me, "Every morning before the girls left for school, we would ask God's blessing, direction and protection for them. Sometimes at night while they slept, we'd stand over their beds and pray for them again.

"If one was having a battle with fear, we'd pray a Scripture like, 'God did not give us a spirit of fear,'" explained the father. This couple had prayed for their children since before conception.

Christian husbands are ideal prayer partners if they're willing and available. But single mothers or wives with unbelieving husbands obviously lack this needed support system. That's why trusted women prayer partners are gifts indeed.

Prized Prayer Partners

For years, I had two prized, dependable prayer partners. Lib was my age, with four children near the age of my three. We prayed every weekday morning over the phone for five minutes at precisely 8:00. When all seven of our children reached those challenging teen years at the same time, we were glad we'd started praying together when they were younger. Now we had more prayer ammunition with which to fight.

We learned new depths of prayer as we went through crises with our youngsters—car wrecks, illnesses, hospital emergency-room trips, minor brushes with the law.

Laura, at the other end of the scale, was my more-mature-in-the-Lord prayer partner. She was five years ahead of me physically and spiritually. Though we lived 40 miles apart, we met twice a month to pray either at her home or mine. She was my encourager, my affirmer, my cheerleader.

"Hey, you're going to make it," she'd often say, laughing about a situation that looked hopeless to me. "Listen, one of my kids went through that pain. I'll help pray you through this. Believe me, it's not as gloomy as you think."

When one of my children was falsely accused, Laura brought me back on course: "That's simply out of character for your child. Don't you believe a lie from the devil. We'll pray and ask God to reveal the truth." She stood in the prayer gap with me for two years until the Lord proved the accuser was wrong.

Then one winter Laura and I, along with our husbands, found ourselves halfway around the world. We couldn't resist the opportunity to go to a special prayer locale.

A Sudden Answer to Prayer

Never before had I heard the depth of wailing, travailing prayer as that offered at the Western Wall in Jerusalem. Here, at the only remains of the wall that once surrounded the temples built in the times of Solomon and Herod, pilgrims—Jewish and Christian alike—come from around the world to pray.

That cold February Sunday I stood there with Laura. As I pressed the names of my children into the cracks of the wall, I prayed softly, "Lord, it's Your will to save. Give my children repentant hearts. Fulfill your destiny in their lives."

Our husbands were on the other side of the dividing partition in the section reserved for men, praying in agreement with us.

Miracle of miracles! Before that day ended, back in Florida, the first of our three children had an encounter with the Lord. Here's how it happened.

Sherry, a senior at Florida State University, was preparing to drive the 125 miles from our home back to campus. A blinding rainstorm delayed her trip, so she drove to the church her Dad and I attended. After circling the building three times, she finally pulled into the parking lot and went inside.

A visiting pastor from Africa was there speaking passionately on the verse, "But seek first His kingdom and His righteousness; and all these things shall be added to you" (Matthew 6:33, *NASB*). Then he added emphatically, *"God has a purpose for your life. Your job is to find out what it is and do it."*

Touched deeply, Sherry began weeping as the Holy Spirit moved with conviction upon her heart. She was about to graduate and she did not know what God's purpose was for her.

My husband and I cried out many times with weeping and petition for our children. God answered mightily.

Steve, another student who had been delayed by the storm, saw Sherry and approached her. Gently but firmly he said, "Sherry, God's not putting up with you having one foot in the world and one foot in His kingdom. You've got to make a choice. I hope it will be tonight."

Sherry broke down. Tears gushed down her face. The battle was over. The Good Shepherd had found our lamb while we were in Israel. He wooed her back through Steve, a longtime family friend.

Right on Schedule

The following weekend, back from our trip, we visited Sherry at her request and attended church together. Afterwards, Sherry asked us to go to the altar and kneel with her. She asked us to forgive her for the years she had opposed God's plan for her life. We wrapped our arms about her and asked her to forgive us, too, for not being the parents we should have been and for failing her so often. We forgave each other.

We still marvel at the way God chose to answer our prayers. Steve was one of the young men in the church for whom I prayed regularly. In fact, I had kept a picture of him in my prayer journal. For eight long years I prayed for him every Friday, while he served in missions in Greece, Germany and Israel and later while he was in Bible school.

What a valuable investment of my time and effort. For years, one of my prayers had been, "God, bring the friends of Your choice into my children's lives." That night God did just that for Sherry. After years of praying, my sudden answer had come!

Sherry graduated from Florida State and enrolled in a Bible school in Dallas. Our other two, Quinett and Keith, came back to the Lord soon afterwards.

You don't have to go to Jerusalem and pray at the ancient Wailing Wall to receive your answer. My husband and I had our own "wailing wall" in our bedroom at home. We had cried out many times—with weeping and petition—for our children. God answered mightily.

Focused Prayer Time

I've since moved far away from Lib and Laura, but we still exchange prayer requests by phone or letter. Too many hours have been invested in our prayer lives together to let distance keep us apart spiritually.

After my husband left the Kennedy Space Center and our family relocated in Northwest Florida, I found two new prayer partners, though it took a while. Fran, more mature in the Lord, brought balance and wisdom to my prayer life. Then there was Carol, who prayed with keen identity since her children were in college or about to launch into their own careers, as were mine.

With these two women I was specific and open about my prayer concerns. I could tell them anything that was on my heart, confident they would share only with the Lord. In turn, I prayed for them during good times and as well as trying times.

We came through several traumas together. Fran's son, Mark, almost died of cancer. Carol, who had already lost one child in a car wreck, spent several weeks on a hospital cot beside her 16-year-old daughter who suffered a broken neck in a smashup. How we praised God for their recoveries!

Other friends were available as intercessors when I needed to call and say, "Please join my husband and me in praying that God will bring victory in our child's situation..." and I'd name that child. Sometimes I asked for prayer from women I knew were prayer warriors without mentioning details of the specific problem or need. I was confident they would pray God's will.

When I joined an early-morning group of six women—appropriately named "the prayer support team"—I was challenged in areas of prayer I'd not yet explored. We met for three years each Monday morning from 5:30 to 6:30 to pray just for our families.

We would walk into Fran's home, get a cup of coffee or cocoa and begin praying aloud. We didn't tell each other our "woes," but took our requests directly to the Father as the others agreed in prayer with us.

How I looked forward to our Monday morning prayer times. I'd usually pace and pray, while others knelt or lay prone on the couch. It was a privilege to pray for each other's children and husbands—and know these women were standing with me in prayer, too.

We experienced wonderful victories. Most of us saw our children make deeper commitments to the Lord during those three years of "focused on the family" prayer time.

After the women left to get their husbands and children off to work and school, Fran and I spent another hour together, praying and talking over our concerns.

Getting Your Husband to Pray with You

By far my best prayer colleague has been my husband. For years we've prayed aloud daily for our children, calling each by name. He'd have favorite Scriptures to pray over them; then I'd pray mine. Together we'd say, "Amen. Yes, Lord, we agree."

"How can I get my husband to pray with me?" women often ask. I usually suggest what other wives have told me worked for them when their husbands were reluctant.

You might say to your husband, "Honey, do you mind if I pray aloud for the children while you say 'amen' in agreement with me?" Eventually he'll get the idea that prayer is just conversation with the Father.

Or if your husband is not sure how to pray aloud, you can give him some Scripture prayers that he can read aloud while you agree. The Psalms are a good place to start.

"Pray aloud?" one mother questioned me, wrinkling her brow in a look of total bewilderment. I knew where she was coming from, because I'd been there once myself. I had to learn to pray aloud as my friends Laura and Lib encouraged me to use conversational prayer. "Talk to God like you talk to us," they'd say.

Parents Pray for Each Other's Children

Some years ago a group of five women in Lexington, Kentucky, read my first book on how to pray more effectively for your children. They went on a mini-retreat to watch an accompanying video I had done. Afterwards, they got the idea to meet regularly to pray for one another's children. Among them they had about 30 children and grandchildren.

"We saw a need to build a wall of prayer around our children, because the enemy obviously was seeking to destroy them. We spent time asking God to teach us how to pray and how to organize," explained Elizabeth, one of the early members.

The women began to meet weekly in local parks and pray for each other's children. Then they were asked to share their vision in local churches, home groups and schools. Because of continued interest, they helped set up several "How to Pray for Your Children" groups. People kept coming back to them with praise reports of fantastic answers to prayers for their youngsters.

Before long, the husbands of the original five women asked if they could pray corporately with their wives. Nine years later their husbands are still involved in this prayer effort.

Gathering at Dorothea and Bob's home one night a week, the group starts off with a covered dish supper, then reports of

> *"We see how much our kids are under attack, and we wonder where they'd be today if we were not committed to continually pray for them."*

answered prayer are shared. Finally the larger group breaks up into small prayer circles to pray specifically for each other's children.

Just before they dismiss, each person takes the name of another parent's child(ren) to pray for in the coming week. Though some of their offspring are now adults with kids of their own, these parents have no plans to stop their prayer group.

Twelve families are currently involved, including three single mothers. Two team couples lead so that if one is out of town, the meetings are not canceled.

Every time I go to Lexington, I meet with them on Dorothea's patio to pray. I always leave excited and encouraged, especially as I've listened to husbands and wives praying for each other's children and grandchildren.

Recently Dorothea and I visited on the phone. "Did your husbands feel uncomfortable praying aloud when they started meeting with the wives?" I asked.

"Yes, praying aloud was a new experience for most of them and they were a bit reluctant at first. Even uncomfortable. But now there is no hesitation among any of us to pray aloud. We see how much our kids are under attack, and we wonder where they'd be today if we were not committed to continually pray for them," Dorothea told me.

The original prayer group has multiplied—spreading into churches in the Lexington area—as praying parents unite to pray for one another's children.

Ask God for a Prayer Support Team

If you don't have a prayer partner, ask God to show you the person who could fill this unique role. Maybe two or three special friends of your same sex could meet with you on a regular basis. I do appreciate the dilemma you may struggle with of finding just the right person to pray with. It may take some time and prayer, but it is worth the wait.

Jesus had 12 close friends, but He had an inner circle, too. Peter, James and John sometimes went apart with Him. They had some memorable times. But don't forget that even those three let him down in the Garden of Gethsemane when He needed them to stay awake and pray with Him.

I want to emphasize our trust must be in God—not in our prayer partners. They may let you down. But God never will.

If you are married to a Christian, ask your spouse to pray with you, starting with just once a week. Then you can gradually find other times to pray together for your family.

I firmly believe that every woman needs a special woman friend (or two or three) with whom she can pray on a regular basis—even if it is just by phone or letter exchange. I send a "prayer letter" to approximately 20 praying friends several times a year, with specific requests to pray for our family. They have volunteered to stand in the prayer gap for us.

How we all need this support! The enemy is relentless in his attempts to "wear down the saints" so we will stop praying and just give up (see Daniel 7:25, KJV). But the good news is this: I believe more and more of us are going to hear of "sudden" answers to prayer.

Remember the incident when Peter was in jail and next on the list to be executed? An angel suddenly appeared to him and said, "Get up quickly." The chains fell off his hands, and he was free. He immediately went to the home of John Mark's mother where an intensive prayer meeting was in progress. At first they couldn't believe it was Peter standing at the gate. I think his sudden freedom was a definite result of those folks praying in agreement (see Acts 12:4-19).

How to Organize a Prayer Support Team

How do you organize a prayer support team? Here are some guidelines that worked for us:

1. Keep the group small (two to six persons).
2. Pray; don't gossip.
3. Start and stop on time.
4. If it's a very small group (two or three) make it all women or all men. A larger group of men and women praying together is fine. An individual prayer partner, other than your spouse, should always be your same sex.

Whatever prayer team arrangement works for your current season of life, do it. Don't wait until you think you will have more time. You won't.

So why not begin now asking God to show you the people to include in your prayer support team? You—and your children—will be blessed. And you will be amazed as you keep a record of the ways God answers your prayers.

God Ordained the Family

In the midst of the praying, it is comforting to remember that God considers families important. Before he called a nation, he created a family. And throughout the Bible, we see His special concern for them.

God chose to send His Son to be born into an earthly family. Jesus knew what it was like to share household chores, live with brothers who didn't understand Him, and be the eldest son to His widowed mother.

God is restoring families today, using His divine order and lines of authority in the process. I believe He is calling us to station ourselves as intercessory sentries, to be watchmen in prayer over our families, seeking His battle plan to thwart the enemy's schemes.

Sometimes in prayer I get a certain strategy—Scriptures to pray—and I ask my prayer partners to confirm it. Together we are then ready and armed to come against the enemy's tactics devised for our family.

Prayer for the Right Prayer Partner

Lord, show me who You want me to pray with on a regular basis. Bring that person's name to my mind and move on her heart if she is to be my prayer partner. Direct me to the specific prayer group I need. May I be an encouragement to those who pray with me. Thank You for those special people You will bring into my life to help me pray for my children. We are believing that You, Lord, will contend with those who contend with our family. In Jesus' name, I ask, Amen.

Prayer of Praise

Lord, help me be a faithful watchman on the wall for my family. Link me with others in prayer who can be intercessors with me. Lord, thank You that You are a faithful God, keeping Your covenant of love to a thousand generations of those who love You and keep Your commands. We know our part is to pray; Your covenant is to answer. How we thank You that You are a covenant-keeping God, faithful and true. Teach us how to pray more effectively as we "stand in the gap" in faith, praying and believing and forgiving our offspring—just as You have forgiven us. In Jesus' name, Amen.

Scriptures You Can Paraphrase or Use for Encouragement

Know therefore that the Lord your God is God;
he is the faithful God, keeping his covenant of love
to a thousand generations of those who love him
and keep his commands (Deuteronomy 7:9).

* * *

I have posted watchmen on your walls, O Jerusalem;
they will never be silent day or night.
You who call on the Lord, give yourselves no rest,
and give him no rest till he establishes Jerusalem
and makes her the praise of the earth (Isaiah 62:6,7).

* * *

The righteous cry and the Lord hears,
and delivers them out of all their troubles.
The Lord is near to the brokenhearted,
and saves those who are crushed in spirit
(Psalm 34:17,18, *NASB*)

* * *

Contend, O Lord, with those who contend with me;
fight against those who fight against me.
Take up shield and buckler;
arise and come to my aid (Psalm 35:1,2).

* * *

But as for me and my household,
we will serve the Lord (Joshua 24:15).

PART II

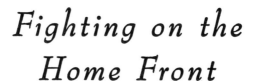

Fighting on the
Home Front

Chapter Five

Praying for Friends and Those in Authority

And the Lord turned the captivity of Job when
he prayed for his friends.
JOB 42:10, *KJV*

Another priceless privilege that comes with praying for your children is praying for their friends, too.

Psychologists agree that nobody influences a teenager—negatively or positively—like his peers. Usually a young person is introduced to his first drug experience by his or her "best" friend. However, a caring friend may also save his life. We need to pray for the right friends to come into our children's lives.

I began referring to this as my "bean-patch praying" after reading how Shammah, one of David's three mighty men, stood his ground in his field of lentils (beans) when the enemy came to attack. His fellow soldiers retreated. "But Shammah took his stand in the middle of the field. He defended it and struck the Philistines down, and the Lord brought about a great victory" (2 Samuel 23:12).

In the back of my prayer diary I started a section titled "Bean Patch," listing the names of my children's acquaintances whom I pray for regularly. Each of us has a different "prayer field," depending on our circumstances. But only the Lord can bring about our needed victory. Our job is to pray, asking in line with biblical principles.

How to Pray for Adverse Influences

Let's consider how you might pray for a child who is being led astray by his or her peers. The following are prayer strategies the Lord has given me for my children at various times. You could adapt them for your children, but also ask the Lord for clear direction as you pray.

1. "Lord, let him see the advice he is getting is foolishness." David, when he believed his son, Absalom, was listening to wrong advice, asked God to "turn [the] counsel into foolishness" (2 Samuel 15:31).
2. "Lord, may my child be delivered from wicked and evil men. God, strengthen and protect my child from the evil one." (See 2 Thessalonians 3:2,3.)
3. "God, you reversed Job's captivity when he prayed for his friends, so I choose to pray for my child's friend who has such a negative influence on him. Bless this young man and let him accomplish your will in his life. May he come to know Jesus as his personal Lord and Savior. I speak blessing, not curses on him." (See Job 42:10; Luke 6:27,28.)
4. "Lord, I believe that until my child is removed from this friend, he will continue to be drawn into the path of unrighteousness. Show my child a way of escape from the bondage of this relationship and pour out your mercy to him/her."

Bless; Don't Curse

One mother almost lost hope for her high-school son, Tommy, as he was being led down a path of destruction by his friend Robert. Then she learned a new way to pray.

"It was Robert who was in favor of skipping Sunday School class and slipping out of church," she said. "He had bought the wine they guzzled down the night we found Tommy passed out on his bed. The alcohol made them sick as overstuffed pups."

She hoped and prayed the hangover and lecture her husband gave the boys would have an effect. But they kept on with their pranks.

"I had to face the fact that Tommy had a will of his own, and chose to do whatever Robert suggested," she shared. "They reinforced each other's worst traits when they were together. I was especially concerned because Tommy had dropped his other close friends just to be at Robert's beck and call."

"Now I pray for all the close friends of my children. But most of all, I've learned to ask God how to pray for them."

Tommy's parents punished, lectured, pleaded, cried, prayed. And prayed some more. They tried to reason with Tommy and Robert together, then separately. Nothing worked, not even forbidding their son to see Robert.

When Tommy's mom had prayed every prayer she knew, she finally asked God to show her how to pray. Lying in bed one evening reading her Bible, she came to a verse in the last chapter of Job. "The Lord turned (broke) the captivity of Job when he prayed for his friends," she read aloud to her husband lying beside her.

"That's what's been missing in our prayers!" she exclaimed. "I think God wants us to pray for Robert as much as for Tommy. Job's friends probably weren't the kind of friends most of us would want."

"Fine. You pray and I'll agree," her husband answered. They asked God to bless, prosper, and direct Robert. No longer did they ask Him to remove this boy from their son's life. They continued praying "blessing prayers" for Robert several times a day.

A few weeks later, Tommy came bounding into the kitchen where his mom was preparing dinner. "Guess what?" he asked. "Robert's got a sports scholarship and is going to college out west."

"But this is January," she said, laying down her paring knife, completely surprised. "I didn't know they passed out scholarships in midterm."

"All I know is he got a phone call telling him he's got one, and he's leaving right away. The college is about a thousand miles from here."

Tommy's parents could hardly believe how quickly God had answered their prayers for Robert. Not only was he blessed with college tuition, but he'd get to play a sport he enjoyed. And, for the time being, he was removed from their son's life. Both young men later committed their lives to God during their college years.

Tommy's mother says, "Now I pray for all the close friends of my children. But most of all, I've learned to ask God *how* to pray for them."

Another mother, whose son smoked pot whenever he got around a certain group of boys, always prayed the same verse whenever she came to our church's prayer group: "Lord, keep my son from the traps set for him by evildoers. Let the wicked fall into their own nets, while he passes by in safety."

Her prayer was a paraphrase of Psalm 141:9,10. One day, when I noticed she was no longer praying that, I asked her about it.

"It was a Scripture I was led to pray at the time," she said. "But those drug pushers leave him alone now, so I don't pray it anymore."

No matter how old our children are, they are influenced by peer pressure. Admittedly, it is difficult to know when to pray for God to remove a person who has a bad influence on your child, and when to pray for that person's best. That's why it is important to ask God how to pray. But it's always appropriate to pray for the individuals to come to salvation.

Here are some prayers we can pray for such people:

Lord, we bless and thank You for our children's friends. May they be good influences upon each other. We know Your Word says bad company corrupts morals. Guard our children from wrong friends, wrong influences and wrong environments. In Jesus' name we ask this. Amen.

* * *

Lord, counteract the influence of the world on my children. Keep them from being misled by wrong peer groups. Plant Your Word in their hearts. Keep me from bitterness when I see them rebel. Give me patience to wait upon Your timing. Show me how to be merciful and gracious even as Jesus was. Amen.

* * *

Lord, help my children choose companions who are wise—not fools, nor sexually immoral, nor drunkards, nor idolaters, nor slanderers, nor swindlers (see Proverbs 13:20 and 1 Corinthians 5:11).

Praying for Authority Figures

As you pray for your children—whether they live at home or away—do you remember to pray for those in authority over them? I'd never thought much about praying for my children's teachers until I heard a pastor stress the need to pray for all those in authority over us. He cited this verse:

I urge, then, first of all, that requests, prayers, intercession and thanksgiving be made for everyone—for kings and all those in authority, that we may live peaceful and quiet lives in all godliness and holiness (1 Timothy 2:1,2).

At the time, my three youngsters were in three different schools with six teachers each. I couldn't possibly know them all personally. But I could lift them up to the Lord in a general way. Not long after I'd added them to my prayer list, our son, Keith, got a telephone call during our supper hour from one of his teachers.

"What did she want?" I asked when he returned to the table.

"Oh, nothing really. She just called to apologize for yelling at me in class today," he said nonchalantly.

Something inside me wanted to shout, "Thank You, Lord! Thank You for showing me the need to pray for their teachers, and for answering those prayers."

Was it my imagination or was there a softening in my children's attitudes toward their teachers after I started praying for them? I was pondering this when our daughter Quinett, who was away for her first year of college, called home unexpectedly at noon one day.

"Mom, my favorite teacher has cancer and possibly is dying. I'm going to the hospital to see her right now. Will you pray for her?" I did right then, as she agreed with me.

Along this line, we need to pray for protection from wrong teaching that comes down to our children from worldly or ungodly teachers. How blessed we are when our children learn scriptural principles from godly teachers who are themselves in submission to the Lord.

Two Christian Mothers Pray

Let me tell you about a prayer partnership of two Christian mothers, Jane and Katie. These neighbors became concerned enough about their children's friends and teachers to find a way to pray for them together.

Every Monday morning for three years they had gone to the high school and then to the middle school their children attended, praying for the teachers, staff and students. One chilly December morning before the sun was up, I rode in the back of the car as they drove to pray at the school sites.

"Between us we have seven children enrolled in these schools," Jane told me. "We feel it's important to pray for the people who daily influence our youngsters."

"Since we began praying three years ago, the drug problem at this middle school is completely gone."

"Sometimes we do spiritual warfare and come against the evil forces that pressure and lure children into ungodly situations," Katie added. "We try to be sensitive and pray as the Holy Spirit directs us."

As these two mothers talked to God out loud in very specific detail, I felt engulfed by the presence of the Lord. Their prayers went something like this:

"Lord, you know Laurie's math teacher, Mr. Smith, is very ill. We understand his cancer may be terminal. Is there something you want us to do for him—besides pray for his healing?"

Silence—complete silence.

Soon Jane spoke up. "Oh, yes, Lord, you want us to volunteer to help in his class. We can do that. And how about Susan's English teacher who has been so out-of-sorts lately? Being short-tempered is not normal behavior for her. Perhaps she has a problem at home. Lord, what can we do for her?"

More silence. Now Katie spoke up.

"You want us to bake her some Christmas cookies and write her a note of appreciation to encourage her?"

"We'll do that, Lord."

After a half hour of prayer for teachers and students at the high school, Jane started the car and drove to the nearby middle school. It was still pitch-dark, and we were the only car in the parking lot.

"Since we began praying three years ago, we understand from the staff and students that the drug problem at this middle school is completely gone," Jane informed me.

"Drug problem gone?" I asked, surprised.

"That's what we've been told—but that doesn't mean they don't need prayer in other areas, or that the drug problem won't return. We are doing preventive praying."

For 30 more minutes these mothers prayed for students, faculty and office staff at the middle school. As mauve clouds whipped across the sky and daylight broke, we headed back to their neighborhood.

"We decided two mothers praying in agreement was better than one praying alone so we spend Wednesday mornings praying just for our families," Katie said. "Besides that we encourage one another and rejoice when we hear prayer answers."[1]

I'd call theirs "bean patch" praying—for they are praying for people who directly affect their children's lives. Katie and Jane are just two of hundreds of mothers who pray for their children's friends and teachers.

One of the best-known groups for praying mothers is Moms In Touch, a California-based organization. These are mothers who come together for one purpose: to pray for their children and their children's schools. No chitchat. No coffee. No snacks. Just prayer. They meet in living rooms or churches across America.[2]

Praying for Employers

Now that my children are out in the working world, I've found it equally necessary to pray for their employers. Doesn't the Bible admonish us to pray for all in authority?

I also pray about the right jobs for them, like this: "Lord, may this child get only the job You want him to have. Open doors that only You can open, and close doors where You don't want him to go. I thank You in Jesus' name, Amen."

The first time I prayed that for Keith, it was the summer before his senior year of high school, and he'd looked everywhere he knew for a job in our small community. Nothing seemed open. Of course, I was praying God would keep doors closed where He didn't want Keith to be. Finally, our pastor told him of a janitorial job in an industrial park. He accepted it, even though he didn't like the sound of the working hours—from 6 P.M. until 2 A.M.

But it proved to be one of Keith's best summers ever. He was free in the daytime to surf the Atlantic, his favorite pastime. And late at night, when he was cleaning windows, mopping floors and vacuuming carpets, Christian men who worked with him talked to him about tithing, giving, praying and other spiritual topics we'd often discussed at our family devotions. But coming from the men he worked with, talking about these things had a stronger impact. How I thanked God for that job and for that special employer who hired Christians.

Many times since then I've prayed, "Lord, open the right doors. Give him a good boss who will give him godly counsel."

Unexpected Answers

One summer I prayed a "door-opening" prayer for his sister, Sherry, and saw unexpected results. She landed a job as a desk clerk at a beach resort hotel. But soon I sensed something was wrong at work. Six weeks later, Sherry came home in the middle of the morning. She'd lost her job. What a blow!

Hadn't we prayed and asked God for just the right job? Yes. Hadn't it been a job that tied in with her planned college major? Yes. What then had gone wrong?

As Sherry fell across her bed crying, I lay beside her, stroking her hair and turning over in my mind some of the negatives of her job. She had to handle several thousand dollars in cash each night, delivering it to the keeper of the safe in the next building. A bit risky for a 17-year-old. Down the beach, two employees had recently been murdered during a robbery. Then there was an employee her own age who had seemed bent on keeping the office in turmoil. I'd prayed several times with my daughter about this troubled girl.

While I was offering a few words of encouragement, my husband poked his head in the door, took one look at us sprawled across the bed, and asked me, "How have you been praying for Sherry?"

"Well, you know that every day I ask the Lord to protect her from evil environment, evil influences and evil people."

"Then why are you surprised she lost her job? Can't you see God's protection over her?"

I got my thinking back into perspective in a hurry!

After the initial humiliation, Sherry forced herself to begin hunting for a job again. Within a week she'd found one. We had almost forgotten about that brief hotel job until the next summer when her former employer asked her to come back to the beach hotel. She declined as she had another job waiting. Had God opened the eyes of this former employer to Sherry's true worth? Perhaps we'll never find out, but it was gracious of the Lord to let us know she had been vindicated in the man's eyes.

Painful as the experience was, we had learned a valuable lesson. Now we can sympathize more readily with those who go through similar disappointments. But in this instance, we believe we also experienced God's divine protection.

Yes, we need to give attention to the apostle Paul's instruction that requests, prayers, intercession and thanksgiving be made for those in authority. Especially for those who wield influence in our own lives and in the lives of our family members.

Watchmen on the Walls

In biblical times watchmen were positioned not only on the city wall, but also in a watchtower located either in a field or vineyard. We who are interceding for our families are modern counterparts to the watchman.

The watchtower was a familiar sight in Jesus' day. At night the watchmen would take turns during various "watches" of the night to guard the field—protecting it from foxes, bears and poachers.

In Old Testament days these towers were used by military watchmen. The soldiers were looking out for the Philistines, fierce bands of renegades who would wait until the crops were ripe, then swoop down to harvest what another man had cultivated.

You may not think your little field is very important. But God has set you in your field as a watchman. Each one of us has a sphere of influence. Most of us don't realize it, but our influence is much larger than we can ever imagine—and will continue on for generations to come, be it good or evil. It's a wonderful responsibility—frightening at times—but wonderful. Always remember, though, you're never in your watchtower alone. Jesus is ever with you, and his Spirit will whisper just the things you need to say and do.[3]

We must take our places as watchmen in the tower where God has placed us, confident that, as we focus our trust upon Him, He will direct our intercession for our families.

Day and night we must be alert to the enemy's plan against our children—whether they are godly or wayward—and join forces with others to pray for them. There has never been a more critical time for parents to be forgiving, loving, praying people. We have a heavenly Father faithful to see us through this high calling.

To contact national groups of women who support and pray for their children, call:

Moms In Touch
P.O. Box 1120, Poway, California 92074
1-800-949-6667

MOPS (*Mothers of Preschoolers*) International
1311 S. Clarkson Street, Denver, Colorado 80210
1-800-929-1287 or 1-303-733-5353

Notes

1. Quin Sherrer and Ruthanne Garlock, *How to Pray for Your Family and Friends* (Ann Arbor: Servant Publications, 1990), pp. 145, 146.
2. Leslie Barker, *The Dallas Morning News* (September 25, 1994), page 1F.
3. Jamie Buckingham, *The Nazarene* (Ann Arbor: Servant Publications, 1991), pp. 87-89. Used with permission of Jackie Buckingham.

Chapter Six

Praying for Wayward Children

*God...grant them repentance leading
them to a knowledge of the truth...
that they will come to their senses
and escape from the trap of the devil,
who has taken them captive to
do his will.*

2 TIMOTHY 2:25,26

The snow was still a foot deep following a freak, three-day winter storm. As my husband drove cautiously down the icy pavement, I spied a little lost black lamb not far from the roadside, bogged down helplessly in the white blanket. "Look, look!" I shouted, as a farmer stomped his way over to the tiny black ball of wool, swooped him up in his arms, and headed toward the nearby farmhouse.

My sagging spirits lifted. We had just spent three days cooped up indoors praying about a troublesome situation in the life of one of our own precious "lambs." God was reminding me once again that Jesus, the Good Shepherd, was out looking for our wandering one. And He's out looking for yours, too.

Finding the Lost Ones

If you have a wayward child, take hope. Believe you'll see that one restored to wholeness, singing praises to Jesus. Hold tightly to that faith. Then read Luke 15—the "lost and found" chapter. You, too, will find reason to rejoice.

This passage has encouraged many downhearted parents. For one thing, it shows us that the Good Shepherd leaves the 99 sheep to go hunting for the lost one. He finds it, heaves it over His shoulder, and brings it back safely. Calling His friends, He says, "Rejoice with me; I have found my lost sheep" (Luke 15:6).

One of the most heartwarming examples of our time has been the restoration of evangelist Billy Graham's son, Franklin. Now an ordained minister serving in missions, this young man was once a rebel. One night while praying for her "lost lamb," as his mother called him, she slipped to her knees to once again commit Franklin to the Lord. She realized she must first "commit what was left of me to God." She did this, then sought God's response.

"He impressed me, 'You take care of the possible, and trust Me for the impossible,'" she said. On the day of Franklin's ordination, his mother shared her story and added, "Today you are seeing the impossible."[1]

"But that was Billy Graham's son," you might say. "What about ordinary people with wayward children?"

I know another mother who never quit praying for her daughter Carolyn, who by the age of 18 had become a popular television model. Disillusioned, the girl turned to alcohol, drugs and sex to find fulfillment. Although she had been raised in the church, she became a drug pusher to support her habits. She turned her back on everything she'd learned, deliberately running from God.

Then one night when she was 39 and completely disgusted with what she had become, Carolyn knelt beside her bed and cried three little words, "God help me!"

"I fell on my knees a sinner and stood up knowing Jesus was my Savior and Lord," she relates. "I ran down to the cocktail lounge where I was part-owner and told everyone in there about Jesus. I never again had a desire to touch alcohol or drugs. In fact, shortly afterward I left the lounge to my partner and moved away to start life over again. My mother had prayed for me for 20 years and never gave up hope. I know it was her prayers that brought me through to repentance."

I later watched Carolyn bring one person after another to the Lord, many of them down-and-outers like she once had been. Through our prayers, mothers, the Shepherd is out wooing our lambs back to the fold—lambs like Franklin and Carolyn.

Prodigals Are Coming Home

As we read on in Luke 15, we come to the story of the Prodigal Son. I call him the "give-me son" because he demanded his inheritance before it was due him. He may have added, "Dad, you can't die soon enough for me. Give me what's mine so I can get out of this dull place."

No amount of pleading, bargaining or threatening would have changed that son's mind. Some of us know what that feels like. We've been wounded by our children. But can we, like the father of the prodigal son, forgive? Can we believe that, regardless of the circumstances, someday we will look out our front doors and see our repentant sons and daughters coming home?

Notice how badly that son "blew it." He went to a distant country and spent his entire inheritance on reckless living. When famine hit the land, he would have gladly eaten the pods offered the hogs, but no one gave him anything. He knew his father's hired servants had it better than he did. So he came to his senses and headed home, willing to be just a servant.

While the son was still a long way off, his father saw him coming. This convinces me that the father believed someday he'd be back. He looked for him expectantly every day. When he spied his wayward son, he was so filled with compassion he ran to meet him, threw his arms around him and kissed him over and over again.

Imagine smothering a stinking, dirty boy straight from the pigpen with love, even before you knew he had a repentant heart. But that's what this loving parent did. What a party he threw! The lost son was found and restored. What rejoicing!

But wait a minute! What about all the money he threw away? What about the heartache and embarrassment he'd caused his father? If we faced similar conditions, could we forgive such a debt?

The focus of the parable is not on the son's actions—it's on the compassionate dad. The analogy is clear: If we want to follow our heavenly Father's example of forgiveness, we must forgive and show compassion for our prodigals just as this father did.

Praying for a Homosexual Son

"Our prodigal made it clear he had rejected our value system when he told us he was homosexual," one pastor's wife said, as she shared the emotional pain she'd felt when confronted by his rebellion. Here is her story:

When you finally learn the truth about your child—usually after having suspected it but not wanting to face it—you are emotionally shattered. The pain is beyond description. You feel you can't talk to anyone for fear other members of the family and colleagues in the ministry will learn the terrible truth.

There were times when I struggled with intense anger toward Ed. I sometimes felt he was rebelling against everything we ever believed in as the ultimate means of hurting us and destroying his dad's ministry. At those times, I was tempted to blame my husband for not being a more attentive father. However, the Lord showed me the true adversary is the enemy of God in Ed's life and in our family—not my son or my husband. My attitude changed.

Later, when we could talk with him without getting angry, I began to empathize with the enormous pain of rejection he had suffered as a teenager. He dropped out of church because he felt he would never find acceptance there. He said the only place he could feel accepted was in the gay community.

"This is the way I am, so you may as well get used to it," he told us. "I wish it were different, but I've felt this way for as long as I can remember. I've asked God to change me, and He hasn't. The unhappiest years of my life were when I tried to deny that I'm gay. Since accepting it, I've been happy. I have a relationship based on mutual respect, not just on sex."

Obviously our son is deceived by the enemy to think he was born like this, because that view is totally contrary to Scripture. But it's useless to argue with him. We can only ask the Holy Spirit to reveal truth to him—which we've done for years. It has been a long, painful battle to pray for him without giving in to despair.

We've learned to lean on God like never before. He has helped us to show love to our son and keep the lines of communication open. The Lord also has provided a few trustworthy prayer partners who are standing with us. Our confidence in His faithfulness is rock-solid, and we refuse to be moved by visible circumstances. While Ed knows that we do not condone his lifestyle, he knows, too, that we love him deeply and have forgiven him. Sometimes he even calls home to ask for prayer.

To other parents suffering this trauma with their children, I can offer this assurance: As they keep their confidence in God, and continue to pray and seek His help to walk in forgiveness, they will begin to see a light of hope at the end of a long, dark tunnel.

The Prodigals Are Coming!

Prodigal children are coming home in droves these days. Some with regret and remorse, but not all with repentance. Some are still strung out on drugs. Some are pregnant, but not married. Most are penniless. Others, with broken marriages, are returning and bringing their children with them, because they have no other place to live.

Every family must decide by seeking God's will through prayer and Bible reading whether to receive a prodigal back into their home. Some families feel the harmful influence on younger children at home is too great a risk. Others allow an addicted child to stay in their home in order to nurse him or her back to health—and to pray "at closer range."

When Jeff became addicted to alcohol and drugs as a young teenager, his mother, Jane, drew closer to the Lord. She and her husband did not feel they should ask their prodigal to move elsewhere.

Often Jane lay on her bedroom floor interceding for him in every possible way. She fasted. She travailed. Sometimes she'd go into his bedroom and pray over the objects he had in his room. Even when he would roar off on his motorcycle, stoned on drugs, she continued to pray this prayer: "God, I free you to do anything you have to do to make Jeff a man of God. God, come and establish your throne in Jeff's life." This is a prayer of relinquishment.

"After praying for months, one day I knew my warfare was over," Jane says. "The burden lifted, although there was no significant change in Jeff. I had that inner knowing that I could stop my deep intercession."

For a while things got worse. Then, when he overdosed on drugs, Jeff sought help. A nearby Christian befriended him, pointed him toward Jesus, and was instrumental in Jane's prayers being answered. Jeff was delivered from his drug and alcohol addiction. Today he enjoys an ongoing relationship with the Lord and is father to a large, happy Christian family.

No pastor, counselor or psychologist has yet been able to explain why some children reared by loving parents with godly values go astray, while others without this nurturing do not. The fact is, some children from Christian homes abandon their upbringing, disappoint their parents and wander in confusion before finally allowing God to guide their lives.

The Occult Nightmare

Several years after having a baby out of wedlock, Jolene came to the Lord and tried to instill Christian values in her daughter Tori. But after learning the circumstances of her birth, Tori rebelled and withdrew from her church friends. She immersed herself in heavy metal music and, later, joined a group of Satan worshipers.

One evening, Jolene returned from her prayer meeting to find an ambulance and police cars in front of her home. Someone had discovered Tori lying unconscious in the street from a drug overdose. They took her to the hospital to pump her stomach, then transferred her to a psychiatric ward for treatment.

This was just one more trauma following many others: Tori slitting her wrists, jumping from a building to attempt suicide, overdosing on drugs, going to a graveyard to conduct mysterious satanic rituals. "When she lapsed into a spell or trance, she exhibited such supernatural strength she would beat me up," Jolene confided.

Friends from her church joined her in intensive prayer for Tori. In some ways it seemed the situation got worse instead of better, but they persisted in prayer. Jolene tried every way she knew to reach out to Tori in love.

One day a 15-year-old boy in Tori's satanic group killed himself. Though Tori also had attempted suicide, her friend's bizarre death so frightened her that she put away all her satanic practices.

"I realized Tori's behavior stemmed from a broken heart," Jolene said. "She was punishing God and me for all the things she'd gone through. When the Lord showed me how deeply hurt she was, I was able to forgive. That brought healing to our relationship."

Tori soon was able to hold a job as a live-in babysitter, and she began attending church occasionally. Jolene continues to pray for her full restoration to the Lord.

> *"She's my prodigal child. She doesn't belong to the enemy. She's coming home someday—to God and to me."*

"She's my prodigal child; she doesn't belong to the enemy," Jolene affirms with confidence. "She's coming home someday— to God and to me."

God Will Restore

Another friend's rebel son ended up in prison. After becoming a Christian, Sondra sought the Lord about him. One day while reading her Bible, this verse pierced her heart: "'Even now,' declares the Lord, 'return to me with all your heart, with fasting and weeping and mourning'" (Joel 2:12).

Through that verse, God shone a spotlight on her heart, revealing her bitterness, anger and unforgiveness. She repented with fasting, weeping and prayer, asking God to change her. A few verses later, she read, "I will repay you for the years the locusts have eaten" (Joel 2:25).

"Even though I hadn't been the kind of parent my son had needed in his growing-up years, God forgave me and placed a promise in my heart," she said. "I trusted Him to restore the years evil 'locusts' had stripped from my life—and to bring my son to accept the Lord."

For Sondra it was a big leap of faith to believe God could reach her son in his prison cell. Today he is still in prison, but he has accepted Jesus as his Lord and plays his musical instruments in the chapel worship services.

Sondra is one of the most joyous Christian mothers I've ever known. What's more, she's a strong intercessor for her state's prison system. She prays for the inmates, guards, superintendent and chaplains. Many parents might be so devastated at having a son in prison they'd never think to intercede for others there, but not Sondra.

She believes some day her son will be released. But her prayer has been answered. The Good Shepherd found her lost lamb, even behind bars.

Hoping for Good News

Rhonda, a 16-year-old junior in high school, was the only one of Nancy's three who was a "problem child." Although she never got in trouble with the law, she continually rebelled against household rules, argued and kept things in an uproar when she was home.

One Friday night, she didn't come home following a football game. Long past her curfew, Nancy called the home of the girlfriend who had picked Rhonda up that evening. Neither of the girls was there.

Saturday morning, the sleepless parents called the police to report the girls missing and the car stolen. For three days and nights, Nancy and her husband, Rick, barely slept. Rick drove around searching during the day, while Nancy stayed close to the phone, hoping for news—hoping, praying and drinking dozens of cups of coffee.

On the fourth day, Rhonda called. "Mom, I'm coming home. Okay?" she asked.

"Yes, yes, come home," Nancy cried. "Where are you?"

"In Pensacola."

"Are you all right?"

"Oh yeah, we're fine. We've been sleeping in the car."

"Please be careful. I'll be waiting for you," Nancy said.

Several hours later, Rhonda came in the front door. Nancy gasped when she saw her—matted hair, wrinkled clothes and bleary eyes. "Honey, we were so worried about you," was all Nancy could manage to say as she hugged her daughter.

But then Nancy fought back anger boiling up within her. *I should be glad she's home, but she doesn't act as if she's done anything wrong,* she fumed silently.

That evening they read that a man suspected of murdering several Florida college girls had been arrested just two blocks from where Rhonda and her girlfriend had been sleeping in the car the previous night. Nancy's anger was tempered by that bit of news. She rejoiced for God's protection over her daughter.

"Lord, How Can I Love Her?"

But she still needed to forgive Rhonda. In church the following Sunday, Nancy talked to God about her feelings. "I don't even like Rhonda," she admitted to the Lord. "She's not pleasant to be around. The house is always in turmoil when she's home. Frankly, I don't think she even cares that she put us through so much anxiety by running away. Lord, how can I love her, let alone forgive her?"

The Holy Spirit's response was almost immediate. In her honest desperation, Nancy opened her heart to God, and He turned back the clock in her mind to see little Rhonda—apron wrapped about her waist—standing on a chair to help her dry dishes. Then she saw a flash of her bundled up with coat and mittens on a winter day, standing in the snow beside the laundry basket, handing Mom her brother's diapers to hang. She had been so lovable then.

She saw her in the second grade bringing home a valentine with her picture on it that showed her grin with a missing front tooth. As the memories paraded through her mind, her heart softened. She remembered how much she'd loved Rhonda.

"Lord, restore that love to me," she prayed. "In the restoring of that love, I know forgiveness will come." As she prayed, God sovereignly flooded Nancy's heart with love for Rhonda. Instant love—almost more than she could contain.

"Not only did I love her, I even liked her again!" Nancy exclaimed. "I forgave her and asked God to forgive me for my wrong attitude."

Nancy's restored love was so important, because Rhonda was one prodigal who returned without any significant sign of repentance. She seemed glad to be back in the shelter of a loving home, but continued doing daredevil things, keeping her parents anxious through her senior year. She went away to college, eventually graduated, and moved to another city to take a job.

"From the day God renewed my love for Rhonda, I was able to respond to her with genuine love and forgiveness," Nancy said. "Somewhere along the way, that love melted her heart. Now when she comes to visit us, she is a loving, caring, appreciative daughter.

"During one visit, she said, 'Mom, I really put you through a lot in my teenage years, didn't I? I never said I was sorry. Please forgive me.' The forgiveness came full circle."

Don't Give Up

Perhaps you are still waiting for a prodigal child to come home. You may look out your front window every day asking yourself, *Is this the day my son/my daughter is coming back from the land of the enemy?* Jesus told us we "should always pray and not give up" (Luke 18:1).

The Old Testament ends with an astounding prophecy:

See, I will send you the prophet Elijah before that great and dreadful day of the Lord comes. He will turn the hearts of the fathers to their children, and the hearts of the children to their fathers; or else I will come and strike the land with a curse (Malachi 4:5,6).

God can restore a wayward child to relationship with his family—if we're willing to love, forgive and keep on praying.

Our forgiveness, however, will never equal that which God offers us and our children, including the prodigals.

Prayer

Lord Jesus, help us to love all our children with Your love and to communicate that love to them. Give us Your wisdom and discernment to help and guide them. Thank You for the assurance in Your Word that nothing is impossible for You (see Matthew 17:20). We anticipate the day when, through prayer and faith, our prodigal, wayward children will turn their hearts toward You. Bring them out of darkness to light; "from the power of Satan to God" (Acts 26:18). We praise You in advance for what You are doing to draw them to Jesus Christ. In His name, Amen.

Note
1. Ruth Graham, "A Mother's View," *Christian Life* (November 1984), p. 52

Chapter Seven

Praying for Stepchildren and Adopted Children

Above all, love each other deeply, because love
covers over a multitude of sins.

1 PETER 4:8

One million new stepchildren are blended into families each year in our nation. Soon one in every three children will be affected by the divorce and remarriage of at least one of their natural parents.[1]

It would be naive to assume these children can go from one family situation to another without carrying their "baggage" of pain and brokenness with them. Compound that factor with the role changes for everyone involved. Children who were once "the kids" become stepchildren, "his" or "hers." Parents who were previously "mom and dad" are now stepparents, "yours" or "mine." The whole new package is fragile at best.

While I was autographing books at a women's conference in New Orleans one fall, an attractive woman pushed a note into my hand. It read, "Last year in Milwaukee, you prayed for me. My stepdaughter has not changed a bit. But I love her as my own. This time last year, I didn't. Thank you for praying with me to forgive her. God did the rest."

Obeying God

Another mother, this time in Florida, stopped me in her church foyer to talk about her struggle to love and forgive a stepson. She tells the story in her own words:

I was forty when I married, and I had no children of my own. Not long after our wedding, Dick, my husband's 17-year-old son, came to live with us. Because his mother was marrying for the third time, she asked us to take him.

We soon discovered that Dick was not only using drugs, he was selling drugs from our house. One weekend, I found five-dollar bills scattered across his dresser. Some boy had come to pick up bags of marijuana and left the money for it.

His father confronted him that evening. "Dick, I know about your drug habit. Though I am not going to turn you over to the law, I will not permit drugs. I love you, and God loves you. But no more drugs!"

Dick left our home, was arrested, and served a three-month jail sentence. He came back and asked our forgiveness, saying he had accepted Jesus. We still sensed an undercurrent of rebellion. In front of other people, he'd say hateful, humiliating things to me.

I prayed long and hard about our relationship. One day, while he was in school, I felt the nudge of the Holy Spirit. "Wash Dick's feet."

"God, are you serious?" I asked. "Do you want me literally to wash this boy's feet?"

All day, I fought the idea. At two o'clock, I gave in. "All right, Lord, if this is what You require, I'll do it. But what if Dick won't let me? He's got his pride, too."

When Dick came in from school, I had a towel and a pan of water waiting in the living room. "Dick, I want to wash your feet," I told him.

"You want to what?" he sputtered, flabbergasted.

"Wash your feet. I have the water here. God wants me to do it. May I?"

"I guess so....I don't understand, but okay."

Slipping off his shoes and socks, I placed his feet in the pan of cool water, gently washing them. Still kneeling, I said, "Dick, I forgive you and I love you."

I dried his feet with a towel, then wrapped my arms around his shoulders in a slight hug. Our eyes locked for one long moment. He picked up his shoes and socks and walked down the hall to his bedroom as if nothing unusual had happened.

He never mentioned our foot-washing afternoon. Nor did I. But because of it, something broke. We both knew a wall between us had tumbled down. He never sassed me again. How beautifully God honored my obedience that hot spring afternoon.

Tenderness, humility and obedience—God wrapped it all up in the single act of foot-washing and used it to blast away the pain separating stepmother and stepson. But the strategy for how to reach him only came when she spent time in prayer, asking God what to do. When Dick reached adulthood, he made a commitment to Jesus—thanks to a stepmother's prayers.

Stepparent Myths

In their excellent book on mending and blending stepfamilies, *Successful Step-Parenting*, Dr. David and Bonnie Juroe, who have eight children between them, dispel some myths about stepfamily situations.

Myth #1: You have to be perfect.
You don't have to be perfect. Instead, recognize your limitations. Realize you are an outsider. Don't have unrealistic expectations.

Myth #2: Children can adapt easily in a stepfamily.
The problem of adaptability is great for those entering into the stepfamily because their personalities are already pretty well molded. The children have developed needs, wants, habits and coping mechanisms that may resist change.

Myth #3: Stepchildren quickly get over loss.
When parents remarry, most children are bound to feel some jealousy and may be envious if the noncustodial parent has bettered his lot in life materially and emotionally. Sometimes the loss of a parent never heals completely; we must respect the child who experiences it.

Myth #4: A stepfamily can operate like a normal family.
A stepparent has assumed the responsibility for helping to raise another individual's children. Most of us have been conditioned to want our own children—not someone else's. A blended family is incredibly more complex because of the stressed emotional relationships.

Myth #5: Stepmothers are wicked creatures.
Stepmothers often become the battleground in the stepfamily. The home always seems to revolve around the mother figure, no matter who she may be. If things go wrong, the stepmother is seen as the culprit. She may be a better cook, housekeeper and friend than the birth mother. However, the key issue is not her ability, but what the children want. Most stepmothers, however, have courage or they would not have accepted their role in the first place.[2]

Displaced Anger

Family counselors tell us that stepchildren bring into a marriage emotions such as anger, fear, rejection, guilt or grief over the loss of their other parent. Reacting from any of these, they may choose the stepparent or stepbrothers or sisters as targets of their aggression.[3]

A teenager may shout, "I don't have to obey you—you aren't my dad!" In some cases, a child may be angry with his or her own parent, but vent that anger toward the stepparent. Leah experienced this firsthand when she married a widower with three daughters.

"The shock of their mother's death and their sudden move to a strange town made the girls emotionally dependent on their father. When he married me, they felt they had to compete with me for his affection," Leah recounted. "I think they were angry at him for getting married again, but they took it out on me. The birth of my own child only created more competition for them."

Leah herself had come from a home where affection and emotional reinforcement were rarely expressed, so she was ill-equipped to give emotional support to her stepchildren.

"I was too inexperienced at the time to realize how desperately the girls needed acceptance and reinforcement," she told me. "I realize now I made a lot of mistakes, and my husband did, too. But we did the best we knew at the time.

"Now the oldest daughter is married and is a stepparent herself, so her attitude toward me has mellowed a lot. During a recent visit I apologized for the hurts I'd caused her and asked her to forgive me, which she did.

"She told me that when her dad married me, she felt he was thinking only of himself and not considering the needs of herself and her sisters. That visit gave me understanding and compassion for what she had been through, and I feel closer to her than ever before. I'm praying the Lord will bring total healing to all three of these daughters."

When a Spouse Rejects Stepchildren

Dozens of mothers have told me a new husband doesn't accept her children from her first marriage. This pits mother and children against the new "head of the house," often causing disruption in family life and division between husband and wife.

Of course, it can be the other way around, too, with the father bringing his children into a new marriage with equal difficulty. "All our fights are about the children," a stepmother admitted.

One husband gave his wife an ultimatum: "If you can't love my children as you would love your own, then I don't want us to have children."

Fear gripped her. "What assurance did I have that I could love his children as much as I'd someday love my own? His

Agape love means loving without hope of receiving love in return. Without this love from God, little hope exists for us as parents or stepparents.

were adolescents, and I wasn't even enjoying them that much, let alone loving them," she told me. This couple opted not to have any children because of the husband's attitude.

Obviously there is no one answer covering all stepparent problems. Forgiveness is essential, but another much-needed ingredient is agape love— God's love, available only from Him. The Word promises, "God has poured out his love into our hearts by the Holy Spirit, whom he has given us" (Romans 5:5). Outside this love from God, little hope exists for us as parents or stepparents.

Agape love means loving no matter what, loving without hope of receiving love in return, loving despite bad behavior. Unconditional love doesn't cut the person off when love is not reciprocal.

Give Up Expectations

Another stepmother told me she finally decided she would stop expecting her stepchildren to love her as much as they love their real mother. "I no longer have those unreasonable expectations of their love," she said, "and it has freed me to be myself."

Still another said, "I got tired of my husband's young son threatening to go back to live with his grandparents, where he had lived after his mother deserted him. The next time he said he was going back to them, I set him on the counter, looked him straight in the eyes and said, 'Murray, you are my son. The only son I will ever have. You can go back and visit your grandparents, but you're never going to live with them again. You are my son, and I love you.' After that Murray never asked to go live with his grandparents."

It's unrealistic to expect your stepchild will love you as much as he or she loves the natural parent, or even as much as you truly love him or her. You may need to surrender that expectation until the Lord performs a heart-change in the child.

Maybe you want to stop right now and pray something similar to this prayer:

Prayer for Blended Family

Lord, with an act of my will, I choose to forgive all in our household who have hurt me. Show me creative ways to express Your love and mine to each child. Lord, You know I sometimes become angry with them. I need to understand life in this household from Your perspective.

Father, help all of us to maintain genuine love and harmony in this home. Show me when to speak and when to be quiet; when to be firm and when to be lenient. Help me to communicate with my children and stepchildren what I am feeling, and let me allow them the same privilege. Thank You for all their positive characteristics and all the potential that is in their lives.

Lord, bless the one who gave birth to these stepchildren. May Jesus be Lord of all our lives. In His blessed name I pray, amen.

The Challenge of Adopted Children

"I'm so grateful to my adoptive parents. Without them, I'd probably have grown up in foster homes all over the state. Besides meeting my physical needs, they gave me their family name, nurtured me with love, and led me to a relationship with God." Adoption at its best!

This adopted son's testimony illustrates what adoption should be. When you adopt a child, you take a stranger into your family as your own son or daughter. The Greek word which is translated "adoption" in the New Testament means "placing as a son," implying that the adopted child has the same rights and privileges as birth children in the family.[4]

The first instance of biblical adoption is recorded in Genesis 48:5, when Jacob took Joseph's sons, Ephraim and Manasseh, as his own. You will remember others: Pharaoh's daughter adopted Moses (see Exodus 2:10). Mordecai adopted Esther, his young cousin (see Esther 2:7). Adoption was not widely practiced by the Jews, but by foreigners or Jews influenced by foreign customs.

A New Testament Picture of Adoption

In the New Testament, adoption is described in terms of a new spiritual relationship. The apostle Paul stated that our entrance into God's family is through adoption (see Galatians 3:26—4:7).

Paul wrote, "He [God] predestined us to be adopted as his sons through Jesus Christ, in accordance with his pleasure and will" (Ephesians 1:5). In Romans 8:15, we read that we have received the right to call God, "Abba, Father"—our daddy. He accepts us into His family like adoptive parents accept a child into their family. We sense His gracious love in a climate of intimate trust and love. Through adoption, God becomes our Father; Jesus, our elder brother.

My friends Beth and Floyd adopted their daughter Sue after she was grown, married and the mother of several children.

Unusual, perhaps, yet they felt God wanted them to do it officially and legally, not just figuratively.

The lawyer handling the case told them, "Though you can disinherit your natural children, you can never disinherit an adopted child. Be sure you won't change your minds about this later." Beth and Floyd assured him they wouldn't change their minds.

"Something broke in Sue when she got the adoption papers saying she belonged to a family," Beth related. "She cried as loving acceptance replaced the pain of rejection. As for our family, we saw again God's love for us, His children. He never disinherits us!"

Special Problems

Parenting, at best, is never an easy job. But as many adoptive parents have discovered, rearing an adopted child often comes with its own special problems and pitfalls. This is not surprising when you think of the variety of reasons children are available for adoption. The most common include illegitimate births, death of one or both birth parents, abandonment and abuse. However, if parents choose to walk in forgiveness, recognizing that God can and will redeem our mistakes, the most seemingly hopeless situations can be transformed into blessings.

Several parents have told me they felt more wounded by their adopted children than by their natural children—possibly because they felt a greater sense of failure as adoptive parents. Some say their failure was due partly to the fact that they had so wanted the adopted children, they may have overprotected or underdisciplined or overcompensated in rearing them. Their good intentions, however, don't change or lessen their hurt.

Lifelong Intercessor

A mother in South Carolina, for example, told me her two adopted teenagers nearly broke her heart with their rebellious actions and their ugly, unkind words. Although she tried to bring them up as Christians, they rebelled and rejected her values.

One day in her prayer time, she complained loudly to God. "Lord, you know how much trouble I went to to get these children. Why are there so many problems with them?"

"If ever I had a clear word from the Lord, it came at that moment," she told me. "He said, *'Not for your pleasure, but for your prayers.'*

"I forgave my adopted son and daughter for their rebellion. I understood that I was chosen to stand as a lifelong intercessor for them. Sometimes I get tired because progress is slow. Yet I praise Him for the 'natural' good I see in them, and I know that, in His perfect timing, we will all be one in the Spirit."

Her discovery should encourage any parent. Whether the child who has hurt you is adopted or is your natural child, look on the situation as an opportunity to be a lifelong intercessor.

Only by the Grace of God

Virginia has also experienced what it means to be a lifelong intercessor. Her 22-year-old adopted daughter, Melody, had three children out of wedlock. Eventually, Melody became a Christian; but before she surrendered her life to Jesus, her parents endured eight years of rebellion, running away, illegitimate babies and a flaunting of all their values.

How did they live through it? "Only by the grace of God poured out on us through prayer, through friends who loved us both and through knowing God was always standing with us no matter what," Virginia wrote me.

"Melody and the babies lived with us most of the time, so it was essential we learn to forgive each other. Though I had always had Melody's best interests at heart, I tried to control her, fearing that if her birth mother had been promiscuous, she might be, too.

"She reacted to my control by rebelling even more. When I saw 'overcontrol' as my sin, I asked God to forgive me. I began releasing her to Him, trusting Him to work in her life."

Virginia said she had to acknowledge she is not responsible for her child's choices. No one can make another person live responsibly.

A Helpful Method

The writer to the Hebrews gives us wise instruction in relationships: "See to it that no one misses the grace of God and that no bitter root grows up to cause trouble and defile many" (Hebrews 12:15).

"That verse taught me that I had to deal with the hurt, resentment and bitterness, or it would eat me up," Virginia continued.

*Godly parenting is not for
the fainthearted. God never promised
it would be easy.*

She wrote out her wrong responses—self-pity, rejection, anger, resentment. Then she would pray, "Lord, I give these to you. Forgive me. I will not justify my wrong responses. Please change my feelings and give me your peace."

"As I forgave my daughter, her boyfriend, and his family, I believe it released grace into my situation so God could work on all of us," Virginia recounted. "Through prayer and lifting to Him each hurt that came to my memory, I was freed to forgive more easily the next time, because the pain of the past was being healed."

Virginia and her adopted daughter are now friends—two adult women who enjoy each other's company.

Godly parenting is not for the fainthearted, and Virginia's experience is a testimony to that fact. God never promised it would be easy, but take heart from this:

He Himself has said, "I will never leave you nor forsake you." So we may boldly say, "The Lord is my helper; I will not fear. What can man do to me?" (Hebrews 13:5,6, *NKJV*)

Charge It to Jesus

Sylvia, another mother of an adopted child, told me about her struggle to forgive her son Matthew. One summer evening she stood at her kitchen door watching Matthew, now 30 years old and married, jump into his compact car and speed angrily down her driveway.

"Why is there always a scene whenever he comes?" she asked herself wearily. Tears flowed down her face as she leaned against the doorway. "Why does he call me names and act so ungrateful about the things I've done for him? I can't seem to satisfy him."

Grabbing her Bible, Sylvia went out to the patio and her favorite lounge chair, the place she often went to pray. "Lord, help me," she cried. "I hurt so badly when Matthew says such ugly things to me. I'm having a hard time forgiving him for all the wounding words."

She began reading the short letter Paul wrote to his friend Philemon to ask him to take back his runaway slave, Onesimus, who had become a Christian. These words of the apostle Paul seemed to leap off the page straight into her heart:

If he has done you any wrong or owes you anything, charge it to me....I will pay it back—not to mention that you owe me your very self (Philemon 18,19).

It was as if Jesus Himself were saying to her, "If Matthew has done any wrong or owes you anything, charge it to Me. I will pay you back. But don't forget, you owe Me your very life."

Those words sparked a practical reaction in Sylvia. That afternoon, she had a long talk with the Lord, charging all Matthew's insults to Jesus' account. "I forgave Matthew and asked God to forgive him, too," she told me. "In doing so, I released Matthew for having consciously or unconsciously inflicted all those wounds on me through the years. Then I thanked God for allowing me to be his mother."

Sylvia learned a valuable lesson we can all benefit from: In our relationships, we must appropriate the reconciling power of the Cross. God purposed that through Jesus all things should be completely reconciled to Himself (see Colossians 1:19,20).

We Did Our Best

One wounded but healing mother of an adopted daughter comments, "I came to the point where I realized God allowed us to adopt this girl. He knew exactly what family to put her into. We did our best in rearing her, and we are not failures as parents.

"We don't need to take on any guilt or shame because she chose to turn her back on us. I'm not sorry we adopted her, for even with the hurts, I still remember plenty of joys."

I don't want to leave the impression that adopted children cause parents more heartache than birth children. Many adoptive parents report that they have no more conflicts with adopted children than with their own.

My friend Fran recalls that some of her most memorable college weekends were those she spent with a classmate from nursing school.

"Though my girlfriend was adopted, she and her mother had a beautiful mother-daughter relationship" she reported. "I saw firsthand what love and acceptance are all about. As a stepchild myself, from a completely different background, it gave me joy to be with that family."

Cross-Cultural Adoptions

Parents who adopt children from another culture face a particularly crucial challenge. They must try to make the child feel accepted, not only by their family, but also by the family's culture and society.

Some parents adopt a child from another culture out of compassion to help the orphaned and homeless. Or perhaps because adoption procedures in this country are so difficult. But then some discover they have problems they can't handle.

One Caucasian family in the northwest United States, with three children of their own, adopted a Latin American child from an orphanage. When he reached school age, they were shocked to have to confront racial discrimination. They never anticipated the problem, and the mother found it impossible to deal with the trauma. The strain caused an already weak marriage to fail.

Feeling the divorce was his fault, the child carried enormous guilt. The father, a doctor, kept the adopted son. The boy is now gaining a sense of acceptance through his father's love and the help of a counselor.

Perhaps prayer, forgiveness and counseling could have salvaged this situation, but their experience illustrates the need for God's direction and help in any decision to adopt children.

The Word of God tells us we can cast all our anxiety on the Lord because He cares for us (1 Peter 5:7). I believe that includes the hurts and heartaches our children have caused us—whether birth children, stepchildren or adopted children.

God not only heals broken hearts, He restores broken families. Stop right now and pray this prayer for your adopted child:

Prayer

Heavenly Father, thank You for the opportunity You gave me to rear this special child, _____ .
Lord, I thank You for the parents who brought him/her into the world, and I ask Your blessing on them.

I thank You for all my child's good qualities: (name them to the Lord). Please forgive me for holding grudges when he/she has disappointed me, disobeyed me or deeply hurt me. (At this point, share with the Lord your innermost thoughts and frustrations about this child. He will understand.)

Father, I choose to forgive _____ , and I ask You to forgive him/her, too. I release my son/daughter to be all you created him/her to be, and I ask Your blessings to rest upon his/her life. In Jesus' name, amen.

If You Gave Up a Child

Perhaps you are a parent who gave up a child for adoption. I urge you to pray for that child and to thank God for the home where he/she is now living. Pray for the adoptive parents. Pray for God's perfect will to be accomplished in your child's life. Thank Him for this child who is able to bless another family.

If you're struggling with guilt, ask the Lord to remove it. You can claim 1 John 1:9: "If we confess our sins, he is faithful and just and will forgive us our sins and purify us from all unrighteousness."

When He forgives you, there is no condemnation. You may need to forgive someone who was involved in the pregnancy or in the decision you made to release the child for adoption. But remember, the key to answered prayer is in harboring no unforgiveness!

Notes

1. Dr. David J. and Bonnie B. Juroe, *Successful Step-Parenting* (Grand Rapids: Fleming Revell, 1983), pp. 9, 19. Used with permission of Baker Book House, P.O. Box 6287, Grand Rapids, MI 49516.
2. Ibid., pp. 20-27.
3. Ibid., p. 35.
4. Herbert Lockyer, Sr., General Editor, *Nelson's Illustrated Bible Dictionary* (Nashville: Thomas Nelson, 1986), p. 20.

Chapter Eight

Praying for Adult and In-Law Children

*We ask God to give you a complete understanding of
what he wants to do in your lives, and we ask him to
make you wise with spiritual wisdom. Then the way you
live will always honor and please the Lord, and you will
continually do good, kind things for others. All the
while, you will learn to know God better and better.*

COLOSSIANS 1:9,10, *NLT*

Do we quit praying for our children when they become adults?
Even if they are walking faithfully with the Lord? No! A thousand times, no! In fact, our godly children need our prayers just
as much as our prodigals do. Why?

When our children are believers—especially when they
become teenagers and adults—the enemy seeks ways to dis-
courage, tempt and trap them and to cause others to speak ill
of them. Because Satan is subtle, crafty and cunning in his
methods, it's important for us to pray a hedge of protection
around our "good" children.

Over the years, many women have shared with me the
prayer battles they've fought for their godly children. Here are
just a few scenarios I recall:

- A daughter with love for God and a zeal for missions was seduced and led astray by a lesbian dorm-mate while away at college. After years of prayer, the young woman is again walking with the Lord.
- A son who had become involved in satanism finally returned to the Lord after years of prayer. Just as he was being reestablished in his Christian faith, a cult group sought him out and is leading him into deception once again. This mother continues to battle and pray for her son.
- A daughter was falsely accused on her job by a jealous coworker and was forced to defend herself before a board of supervisors. After much prayer, she was vindicated.
- One mother was so disillusioned when her son married a foreigner and embraced her false religion, she gave up praying for him. But I challenged her to consider how praying for both of them could make a difference, and she decided to pick up her prayer sword once again.

Examples for Us to Follow

Jesus knew Peter would fall into temptation and deny that he knew his Lord. But rather than being angry with Peter, Jesus simply said to him, "Simon, Simon, Satan has asked to sift you as wheat. But I have prayed for you, Simon, that your faith may not fail. And when you have turned back, strengthen your brothers" (Luke 22:31,32).

Before He went to the Cross, Jesus specifically asked the Father to protect His followers from the evil one, and to keep them in unity so the world would know God had sent Him into the world (see John 17:6-21). If Jesus prayed this way for His spiritual children, we as parents should follow His example and pray in a similar way for all the children God gives us.

My good friend Beth prays daily for each of her four daughters, their husbands and her 14 grandchildren, calling each by name. One particular prayer she always prays is that they not be deceived, that they not walk in error, and that they be counted worthy to stand before the Lord at His coming.

We find in Scripture many prayers that Paul prayed for his spiritual children—including the passage from Colossians cited at the beginning of this chapter. For the believing saints in Ephesus, Paul prayed, "I keep asking that the God of our Lord Jesus Christ, the glorious Father, may give you the Spirit of wisdom and revelation, so that you may know him better" (Ephesians 1:17).

What a wonderful thing to pray for our own believing children! They could attain no higher reward than to receive wisdom and revelation from God and come to know Him better. Surely, such children will make a difference for godliness in this world.

Paul's prayer continues in Ephesians 1:18,19—also a good example for Christian parents to use as a guide:

> I pray also that the eyes of your heart may be enlightened in order that you may know the hope to which he has called you, the riches of his glorious inheritance in the saints, and his incomparably great power for us who believe.

In a time when there seems to be so little hope, we need to pray that our children may know the hope to which they have been called. They need to see that this life is not all there is—but they are already rich because of what they are to inherit. They are the heirs and heiresses of the kingdom of God.

Susanna Wesley was a woman of action, a strict but fair disciplinarian and a woman of prayer. It is said that she prayed daily with each of her 10 children as she reared them. (Though she had 19, only 10 survived.) But she also knew the importance of consistent, daily prayer in the lives of her children after they were grown. Little wonder that two of her sons—John, the preacher, and Charles, the hymn writer—had such a profound impact on the Christian world.[1]

Praying for Our Children's Spouses

A mother's prayers for her married children naturally include their spouses, too—prayers for right career choices, for fellowship with believers, for godly homes, for God's direction, guidance and wisdom in every endeavor.

After graduating from college and working for a Christian magazine, our son, Keith, attended Bible school where he met his future wife, Dana. One day Keith told his fiancée, "You are a jewel, a real treasure. My mom prayed for my future wife for years. She didn't know your name, but she was covering you with prayer."

A log-sized lump jammed my throat when I found out Keith had said that to Dana. I remembered his rebellious years when I wondered if he knew, or cared, that I was praying for his future.

Another time, as we comforted our daughter after she broke off an engagement, we marveled at her ability to go on with God and not look back. Eventually she wrote a prayer asking the Lord to bring His choice for a husband into her life.

In the meantime, her dad and I returned wedding gifts, sent out announcements that the wedding was off, and tried to keep level heads about it all. With God's help we made it through yet another family crisis, while at the same time learning more about how to pray for our children. Today Michael, our son-in-law, is a special part of our family.

Affirm Them Often

Frankie, the keynote speaker at a large Christian women's meeting, started to tell the story of her son's recent miraculous healing when she paused and motioned for a woman in the front row to come to the platform.

"I want to introduce my wonderful daughter-in-law, Katnryn," she said with pride. "She has been a faithful wife who stood by my son during his critical illness, and I greatly appreciate her."

The young woman held her head a bit higher and threw her mother-in-law one of the biggest grins I'd ever seen. I watched, puzzled, as Kathryn returned to her seat.

I knew the two of them had not had a close relationship. In fact, they were often worlds apart. Kathryn had met Frankie's son, Ralph, at the beach soon after he'd divorced his first wife,

Accept your in-law-children as they are and be an emotional and spiritual support.

and they rushed into a marriage that Frankie and her husband openly opposed.

"What prompted you to recognize Kathryn like that?" I asked Frankie afterwards. "I thought you'd had a problem accepting her, especially since you wanted your son to marry a Christian."

"While preparing my speech, God dealt with me about my judgmental attitude toward Kathryn," Frankie admitted. "Remember how I used to complain about her? When He pointed out my sin, I knew I was guilty; I had judged her many times. I asked the Lord to forgive me, and I made a decision to forgive Kathryn. The Lord wanted me to recognize her publicly to affirm her for her positive qualities."

From that day on, Frankie went out of her way to affirm her daughter-in-law, and they began to enjoy a more harmonious relationship. The secret? First, Frankie responded to the Holy Spirit's nudge and repented for her judgmental attitude. Then she decided to accent the positive instead of dwelling on the negative and chose to forgive Kathryn. Since then her daughter-in-law has given her heart to the Lord and they have a solid and happy Christian household.

"We have to accept our in-law-children as they are and be emotional and spiritual supports," one mother-in-law wrote to me.

Misunderstandings and Hurt Feelings

Here are a few of the grievances I've heard from women about their in-law children:

- A son-in-law who allows his wife to visit her parents only once every two years, even when a free plane ticket is offered.
- A daughter-in-law who insists on spending all the holidays with her family, never with his.
- A daughter-in-law who never invites her husband's parents for a meal, though they frequently invite her and their son for dinner.
- A son-in-law who insists on handling the finances, including his wife's earnings, and squanders the money on his own selfish interests.
- A son-in-law who accepts a down-payment on a house from his wife's parents, but shows no gratitude for the gift.
- An in-law child who won't allow his spouse any contact with her family or former friends.
- An in-law child who influences his/her spouse to stop attending church.

These days, young people often meet their future mates at college or after taking an out-of-town job. The in-law child may come from a totally different background than that of the family back home. Often both sets of parents have big adjustments to make.

In Bible times, families were generally more closely knit than in today's Western cultures, and parents had a strong say-so in their child's choice of a mate. Also, since a girl often married at an early age and either lived nearby or with her husband's family, her mother-in-law customarily continued the training her own mother had begun.

A strong and loving bond sometimes developed between these two. Naomi referred to Ruth, her widowed daughter-in-law, as "my daughter." Let's reflect a moment on Naomi and Ruth's special relationship.

Biblical In-Laws, Naomi and Ruth

When famine hit Bethlehem, Naomi's Hebrew husband moved his family to Moab where food was more plentiful. Their two sons married Moabite girls, Orpah and Ruth (see Ruth 1).

Problem: Moabites were foreigners to the Jews and, while marriage to Moabite women was not forbidden, any sons of such marriages were not fully accepted into Jewish religious practices (see Deuteronomy 23:3).

We are not told what resentments Naomi may have felt toward her sons for marrying aliens or toward her foreign daughters-in-law. She may have struggled with it. However, the very close bond between Naomi and Ruth indicates Naomi had come to a position of acceptance.

After the death of her husband and her two sons, Naomi decided to return to Bethlehem. Ruth's attachment is apparent in her powerful declaration, "Where you go I will go, and where you stay I will stay. Your people will be my people and your God my God" (Ruth 1:16).

Here was a Gentile woman committing herself to her Jewish mother-in-law and to the God of the Jews. Her scrupulous obedience to Naomi's guidance eventually resulted in Ruth's marriage to Boaz.

When their son Obed was born, friends said to Naomi, "Your daughter-in-law, who loves you and who is better to you than seven sons, has given him birth" (Ruth 4:14,15). What a tribute! To be given seven sons was considered by the Hebrews to be a great family blessing; to have Ruth as a daughter-in-law was judged to be the equivalent! The story of Naomi and Ruth is a glorious example of covenantal love between in-laws.

Focus on Good Qualities

One afternoon I stopped by to visit my friend Norma while passing through her town en route to a meeting. As we sat at her kitchen table sipping herbal tea, we began to share about our children.

Norma admitted it was difficult to accept her three young daughters-in-law. All lived nearby, so she couldn't avoid noticing their weak characteristics. One was always late. Another watched too many soap operas. Another was a "mama's baby," always running home when she got miffed.

I shared my friend Frankie's experience and how she now looks for "plus" traits in her daughter-in-law. "Do you feel you need to forgive your sons' wives?" I asked. "Maybe you should thank God for some of their good qualities and commend them for those things."

Norma was open to the idea. Before we'd finished our tea, she bowed her head, forgave each daughter-in-law, and thanked God for these special young women her sons had married.

In the following weeks, Norma continued to thank Him for her daughters-in-law and for their virtuous attributes. They are good cooks and homemakers. They love their husbands and try to cooperate with their plans to go camping, hunting and fishing. Two of the three attend church on Sundays. Each of the three has many positive traits. She simply needed to look for them. Norma phoned a few months later, ecstatic about the improved relationships with her daughters-in-law. They had begun sensing Norma's acceptance. No doubt her willingness to forgive and to look for their positive qualities has made a difference in this family's in-law relationships.

Forgive My Son-In-Law?

A woman who heard me speak at a retreat about our need to forgive our children asked afterward, "Must I forgive a son-in-law, too?"

'Yes, of course, when that's needed."

"Mine's committed a horrible crime. It's been in all the newspapers. If he goes to prison, I'll probably have to take care of my daughter and their children. It's so hard to forgive him."

As we prayed, it became apparent she was mad at God. She blamed Him because her daughter had married a man the mother considered a bum. Why hadn't He protected her from this terrible mistake?

As we talked, she realized she needed to release God from her judgment, forgive her daughter for marrying the man, forgive the son-in-law who had disappointed them, and ask God to forgive her for her bitterness and anger. She bowed her head and, through tears, relinquished the "whole package" into the Lord's hands.

"There, it's done," she declared. "He's forgiven, and I'm forgiven. And I trust God with the future." Of course, the road ahead of her is still difficult because of the seriousness of her son-in-law's crime. But now she can walk that road with God's strength and enablement—and without the additional burden of bitterness and unforgiveness.

Another Culture

When your child marries someone from another culture, you may have an especially difficult time understanding your in-law child, as Belle, a recent widow, experienced.

Her son Kirk married Lu, an oriental divorcée, when he was with the Air Force in Hawaii 12 years ago. While living in Germany and Las Vegas, their marriage was relatively stable because they enjoyed the company of many military couples like themselves. When Kirk left the military and moved to fiorida, his wife discovered a whole community of war refugees from her country. As Lu spent more and more of her nights playing cards and gambling with this group of people, tension built in their marriage.

Whenever a feud breaks out between Lu and Kirk, their six-year-old daughter is sent to Grandma Belle's. Sometimes she stays overnight; sometimes she stays several days. On occasion, when Lu is quarreling with Kirk, she herself may come and stay at Belle's home, bringing with her deep-seated fears of evil spirits lurking in the dark, her ancestor worship, and her belief in reincarnation. Some of her unusual habits are based on superstition; some come from fears she picked up during the war when she was the only member of her immediate family to survive.

Don't Tell Them How to Live

Belle decided long ago she wouldn't tell her children how to live. She accepts them and their spouses just as they are, even when she doesn't approve of their ways.

When Kirk's best friend died of cancer, he went to help the wife straighten out her legal papers and to do some house repairs for her. Lu became insanely jealous. In a fit of rage, she threw Kirk's clothes out, gathered up her jewelry and ran screaming into Belle's house to tell her how awful her son was. "I'm leaving him, and I've got my jewelry to sell for money to survive on," she shouted.

After a brief chase down the driveway, Belle grabbed her arm and spun the tiny woman around. She looked her in the eye and said, "Lu, I'm the only mother you have to love you. Stop this foolishness. Kirk is not interested in that widow. He only wants to help her. He'd want his best friend to do the same for you, wouldn't he?"

Lu broke into sobs. She agreed to take her daughter, go home and return Kirk's clothes. They have since put their marriage back together. Kirk, though innocent of any wrongdoing concerning the widow, asked Lu to forgive him.

"Now that I've accepted Lu as she is, it makes forgiving a lot easier," Belle confided to me. "Because of cultural differences, I still find it hard to understand some of her ways; but I am committed to be a loving mother-in-law to her."

Teach Younger Wives

Ever watch a mother cat or dog defend her babies? Nature's example is graphic: *You touch my offspring, and you deal with me.* We human parents tend to bristle the same way when one of our children is "attacked." But such a response in an in-law situation can wreck a relationship.

My friend Judy discovered a way around this problem when her daughter-in-law, Toni, kept criticizing Judy's son. Instead of silently brewing over the attacks, Judy directly, but gently, challenged her son's wife. "Don't you ever do anything wrong?" she asked. "I know I'm lacking in many areas of my life. It's self-righteous for us to exalt ourselves above our husbands."

I was surprised at the openness in the relationship. "Doesn't she resent your being so direct?" I asked.

"No, not really," Judy answered. "We have a healthy relationship. She allows me to help her work on areas where she needs improvement, but I only do it when I see she is out of line with God's standard. We read the Bible together to find an answer to whatever is troubling her. The apostle Paul told the older women to train the younger women to love their husbands and children. I try to do that since Toni doesn't have her own mom now."

"You two have an unusual relationship!" I remarked.

"Maybe so. We don't ignore our differences; we talk them out, either by phone or person-to-person," Judy said. "I forgive her every time a hurtful situation comes up. If she keeps on talking against my son, I will remind her that the Bible says, 'Bear with each other and forgive whatever grievances you may have against one another. Forgive as the Lord forgave you'" (Colossians 3:13).

"I Long to Find My Grandson"

On one of my speaking trips, I stayed in the home of Lydia, a widow whose son was kidnapped and murdered on his way to work a few years ago. Her former daughter-in-law won't let her see her grandson, though they live in a neighboring town. Naturally, her heart aches.

"Forgive her? Yes, I've forgiven her, and I pray for her every day," she said sadly. "But I long to hold my grandson. He looks so much like my son, and it would give me comfort to have him visit me, if only once a year. All my letters and packages to him are returned. But that doesn't erase the fact that he is my grandson. Maybe someday, when he is older, he'll find a way to come and see me."

Mothers like Lydia are not isolated cases. There are hundreds of mothers whose former in-law children deny their offspring the privilege of knowing grandmother and granddad, creating yet another need for grandparents to forgive and continue praying for God's intervention. Someday, I hope to hear that Lydia's prayers have been answered.

Love Never Fails

"Love never fails," Paul wrote to the Corinthians. "These three remain: faith, hope and love. But the greatest of these is love" (1 Corinthians 13:8,13). Getting along with in-law children is smoother sailing when we exhibit all three.

I was visiting my friend Bettye, enjoying pumpkin pie and coffee together just after her son and family had left from their Thanksgiving visit.

"It would be natural for me to get upset," she said, sharing about her relationship with her daughter-in-law. "She's started taking my grandson to a religious group that my husband and I don't approve of. When I start to react, the Lord reminds me, 'You just love her!'"

"Is that hard to do?" I asked.

"Sometimes it is," she said, nodding. "But when I draw her in as a part of my treasured family and treat her in a loving way, she responds with warmth and tenderness. She's my son's wife and the mother of my grandchildren, so I'm trusting the Lord and keeping my mouth shut about her false religion. She knows that we believe Jesus Christ is the Son of God and the only way to obtain salvation."

Bettye stopped to refill my coffee cup, then continued. "At first, I was hurt that she is exposing my young grandson to her false teaching. But I have been able to forgive her. God requires from me faith, hope and love. That's what I'm counting on to see me through. Love never fails; it always wins!"

I believe Bettye is right. She's found an unbeatable solution to in-law problems.

Let's believe that it is God's will for our children's spouses to be saved, and surrender them to the Lord. We must be assured that He will draw them to Himself because we have entrusted them to Him. Again, we can leave up to God the time and the way He works in their lives.

Prayer for Adult Children

Father, I bring to You my adult children, _____ (name them). They have heard the Word of God, which I've taught them, and they believe in You. Now protect them by the power of Your name, Lord Jesus. Don't let the evil one steal from them the truth they have received, but rather let integrity grow in them. Make them mighty men and women of God to Your honor and glory.

I pray my children will be delighted in You, Lord. May they commit to You everything they do, trusting You to direct their every step. Continue to fulfill Your will for them, in them and through them. Give them keen discernment so they will not fall prey to Satan's tactics nor entertain his lies in their thoughts. Lord, I pray they will always desire to please You instead of pleasing people. Thank You for Your faithful care over my children. Amen.

Prayer for Children's Spouses

Lord, thank You for my children's spouses. Help me to love and accept them just as they are. When I am inclined to judge and criticize them, remind me I am not always lovable either. My own children have character weaknesses which I tend to overlook when an in-law child is involved.

Teach me how to pray more effectively for my children's mates. Help me to affirm them for their good qualities much more often. When they ask for advice, give me godly wisdom in how to respond. Lord, I so want to love them with Your love shed abroad in my heart—which is a gift of the Holy Spirit (see Romans 5:5, *KJV*). Enable me to be a good in-law parent. In Jesus' name I ask. Amen.

Prayers After a Divorce

Dear Lord, it is difficult to pray for an ex-son-in-law who has left my daughter for another woman. I know I am to stand in the gap for my grandchildren's father. I admit it is hard. Help me walk in forgiveness so my prayers will not be hindered. Turn this man's heart toward You. Help him be a good father, though he chose to move far away from his children. Heal my daughter from her broken heart. Give her assurance of Your love and acceptance. Lord, we all need patience and Your guidance in getting us through this family crisis. We cry out to You for mercy and grace. In our Savior's name. Amen.

* * * * *

How my son is hurting, Lord. She betrayed him, and he is devastated over her leaving. I pray You will bring her from deception to the truth of what she has done. It is not too late for a reconciliation.

"Open [her] eyes and turn [her] from darkness to light,

from the power of Satan to God, so that [she] may receive forgiveness of sins and a place among those who are sanctified by faith in [Christ]" (Acts 26:18). Lord, intervene in their lives. Show Yourself strong on their behalf.

* * * * *

Lord, my child was wrong to walk away from that marriage. I hurt so for my ex-in-law child. Teach me how to pray for both parties. I can hardly see beyond my own pain. But You are the mender of broken hearts. You are the Redeemer, the Deliverer, the Savior. I cry out for Your healing grace to see us through this painful period. Oh, Jesus, come with Your peace. Good Shepherd, cradle us in Your arms. Woo my child back to You! You are his/her only hope. Amen.

* * * * *

Oh God, we didn't know. She married a controlling and manipulative wife abuser. Help our son-in-law realize he needs professional counseling and deliverance. May he turn his heart toward You, Lord. Cause good to come from what the enemy meant for evil in our daughter's life. At the moment, I don't honestly see how it is possible. But I do know nothing is impossible for You. Help, Lord, help!

Note
1. Arnold A. Dallimore, *Susanna Wesley* (Grand Rapids: Baker Book House, 1993), p. 131.

Chapter Nine

Praying for Special-Needs and Dying Children

There is a time for everything...
a time to be born and a time to die.

ECCLESIASTES 3:1, 2

"You are a special mom if, without bitterness or rebellion, you can see your handicapped child as God's special gift to you," says the mother of a child with cerebral palsy.

This mom, who has three active, healthy children and a young son with a crippling disease, shares how she prays for him. She prays "that other children will accept my child and will try to be his friend, though he is different; for wisdom and unending patience for myself, our children and our enlarged family; that my son's life will glorify God on earth by completing the work God has given him to do (see John 17:4); and for his life to touch others. Yes, I pray for his healing, and I wait."

I'm sure God has placed similar prayers in the hearts of thousands of other mothers who, like this one, has a special child to love, care for and nurture in prayer.

She Prays for Her Adult Daughter

Christine, whose husband lay in a coma for 13 years before he died, has a 45-year-old retarded daughter, Karen. The daughter lives 400 miles from home with the supervisor of the day-care center where she is employed. Every day, Christine thanks God for providing for Karen's needs.

"The Lord has been gracious in sending people who now accept Karen and give her the opportunity to be as productive and well-adjusted as she is," Christine said. "She loves working with the babies and toddlers in the center. She rocks them, changes their diapers, sings to them and prays with them. What's more, she makes a salary that lets her pay room and board to the family she lives with. She rides the bus to work and, on Sunday, walks to a little church down the street."

Karen realized she was severely rejected by other people—even by those in the small-town church her family attended. But she knew Jesus wouldn't reject her. Christine taught her that truth.

"This girl talks to Jesus about everything, and He tells her what to do," Christine said. "It's beautiful to see her childlike faith, her devotion to the Lord. Accepting a child like Karen is, I think, the first step to wholeness for a mother with a disabled child."

Born with Down's Syndrome

When Ellen's grandson was born with Down's syndrome, she wrote her prayer in her journal:

Thank you, Lord, for this chance to stretch some more in Your direction—to trust You when I cannot understand. Help me get my eyes off people and myself, and onto Jesus and His eternal, long-range view. He has the tele-scope. I have a chance to see how God sees people. Not by how much they can do, say, write, contribute. He loves us—me—Jason—just because we're people, made to reflect His glory. Jason and others like him offer me—us—a chance to be compassionate and loving, not mean, narrow, bigoted or selfish.

She later wrote me, "This experience caused my faith to enlarge. All during Jason's first year of life, the Lord highlighted verses about seeing as He sees, speaking as He speaks, doing what He does. Using God's eyeglasses. He's enlarging my range of vision. Everything around me changes, but God Himself and His law are more sure than any law of physics."[1]

Most of us probably know parents of a child with special needs who could use our undergirding prayers and support. A promising Scripture for all of us reads, "I know whom I have believed, and am convinced that he is able to guard what I have entrusted to him for that day" (2 Timothy 1:12).

A New Level of Praying and Learning for Parents

My writing mentor and friend, author Jamie Buckingham, wrote the foreword to the first edition of this book. I wanted to share Jamie and Jackie's prayer journey on behalf of one of their children. Jamie went to his heavenly reward in 1992, but the son he writes about here is doing well.

When we realized our number four child had a reading disability, he had completed his first year in school and it was obvious something was wrong. We enrolled him in a Christian school where he repeated first grade. It was a disaster. He was no further along than when he was in kindergarten.

We had him tested. Although he had a high IQ, the tests indicated he had certain learning disabilities which hindered him in reading and writing. We put him under a reading specialist, had him tutored, sent him to clinics and put him in glasses for a year. We enrolled him in a class where he spent agonizing hours putting pegs in holes, walking balance beams and crawling under ropes stretched low to the ground. We even took him to a Kathryn Kuhlman healing service. Nothing seemed to be working.

Although he was back in public school, the teachers didn't do much with him but advance him along with the class—even though he could barely read and write.

When he was in the fourth grade, I realized I could not depend on anyone else to help him. It was up to God. And me.

My part was to pray. God's part was to heal.

Gradually I came to understand that while God could heal my son instantly, He had more in mind. He wanted to teach me how to pray for my son—and He wanted my son to learn how to receive my love and appreciate my prayers. For the next 10 years I never missed a night, if I was home, of going into his room when he went to bed, sitting on the side of the bed and talking and praying with him.

The talking was important. I wanted him to know that regardless of the fact he had a problem, his mom and dad—and his brother and sisters—were proud of him. We did not blame him for his problem, nor did we see him as being different from the other children. In our eyes, he was simply our son.

If he'd had a bad day, I encouraged him. I wanted him to know he was loved and needed and appreciated in our family. I wanted the last thoughts to enter his mind before he went to sleep—the thoughts which would influence his subconscious during the night hours—to be positive thoughts.

But I am convinced that while the parental encouragement kept him well-adjusted socially and drew him into a deep love relationship with the family, it was the prayers that brought the healing.

He finished high school, thanks to a splendid teacher who took him on as a special project and helped him graduate—even though he was only reading at a fourth grade level. Two years later he came to me and said, "Dad, I'll always be a common laborer unless I go to college like the other kids in the family. I want to enter agricultural college and learn to work with animals."

Again, we encouraged him, even though all the odds were against him. This time my wife and I had to pray for him in absentia as he struggled, along with his faithful wife, to master textbooks on horticulture, animal anatomy and farm management by listening to tapes. But he persevered. And God answered our prayers.

When he graduated, he was reading at college level. Soon he had a fine job as a ranch manager, responsible for prize animals worth thousands of dollars each. Proud of our son? You bet! But far more, Jackie and I are grateful to a loving and faithful God who answers the prayers of parents for children.

Today, Jackie says, their son has his own irrigation company and manages a horse boarding farm. God faithfully answered the prayers of a mother and father, maybe not in the way they envisioned, but in His way and in His timing.

A Struggle Against Anger

Corine is an engineer's wife who has suffered many bitter disappointments involving her seven children—from mental illness and drugs to cult involvement. But she has learned to walk in forgiveness. When her daughter Betina was born and Corine learned she was underdeveloped mentally, she was mad at God.

"When she turned three, I finally decided I must accept Betina," Corine shared, as we visited at a women's meeting in Denver. "I had loved her since birth, but accepting her as mine—that was a different story. I finally forgave God for my disappointment in Him. I forgave Betina for disappointing me, and I accepted her as my own."

Coping with Betina has not gotten easier. She now has the body of an adult but the mind of a child. Currently she is

"I believe God will use each of my children as He did the loaves and fishes— to feed multitudes. Right now, some of them are in the breaking process."

obsessed with marriage. Her younger sister is planning a wedding, and Betina fantasizes about a handsome young man who lives nearby. When she sees him and his girlfriend, she throws a temper tantrum. One day, in a fit of jealousy, she smashed the front window of his home.

"Such situations are really embarrassing," Corine said, "and I have to struggle against anger. I have to stop it the minute it surfaces or it would give way to unforgiveness."

Whenever she loses her patience and says something that upsets Betina, Corine immediately says, "Oh, darling, I'm so sorry. Will you forgive me?"

Sometimes Betina stares at her and says, "No, today I will not forgive you."

"But Bet, if you love Mother, you have to forgive," Corine responds. "Remember, Jesus requires you to forgive me and me to forgive you. We can't do anything else until we forgive, so let's sit down and have some tea and forgive, okay?"

It sounds easy, but it isn't. Sometimes Betina argues for hours, "No, Mom, I will not forgive." Over and over, Corine prays for patience, knowing she must set the example for her special daughter.

God has a purpose for Betina, and Corine is trusting Him to bring glory from her life. She is trying to teach Betina that getting married is not the ultimate measure of success in life. "Betina loves the Lord and has a personal relationship with Him. I just want her to see that no one can love her as He does," she told me. "I have five sons and two daughters, and I believe God will use each of them as He did the five loaves and two fishes—to feed multitudes. Right now, some of them are in the breaking process."

If there is one statement I've heard from every parent who shared with me the heartache and disappointment of a mentally underdeveloped child, it is this: "I have learned to walk in forgiveness daily!"

Getting a Word from God

How do you choose between helping a child fight to live and finally relinquishing him to death? When do you cross the fine line between those choices? One mother chose to help her 13-year-old daughter, Lisa, fight to live because she felt God had led her that way.

When Lisa's severe headaches turned out to be symptoms of a life-threatening disease, her mother simply would not accept the doctor's report that her child had a slim chance of recovering. "They told me what they knew in the natural, but in my heart I had God's word to me."

During the daytime, Maureen stayed close to Lisa's hospital bedside, reading encouraging Bible passages aloud to her. Over and over, she told Lisa how much she loved her. Although Lisa was in a semi-coma, her mom told her all about the family's activities as though Lisa understood every word. The last I heard from this family, Lisa was still alive—with her mother's prayers encouraging her.

"I believe all our trials are designed to make us better, not bitter—to make us press towards God, not away from Him," Maureen said. "Out of every dark experience comes a happy result. God's mercy and grace have been on me and my family through this."

Unexpected Death

Our times are in God's hands. Mothers who have seen their own children die tell me they initially felt anger—at God for not stopping it. At the drunk driver whose car hit them. Even at themselves for not being able to somehow intervene.

One Mom, still angry at God some months after her son's untimely death, went to a mountaintop to pray. She began to shout at God over and over, "Why my son? He was a wonderful son! Why my son?!"

As she quieted down, she sensed God echoing back to her, "Why My Son?"

The words hit her heart with their arrow of truth. God gave His Son—He didn't stop Him from death on the Cross. She began to sob. At that moment, her healing and restoration began. Her son was with God's Son in heaven.

Yes, our times are in the hands of a loving Father who sees beyond our own understanding. We cannot on this side of heaven explain some things about the death of those so young.

His Life Counted

When Mark, a 21-year-old friend of one of my children, died from a disease that had plagued him since birth, I wrote his mom a note. Her response was one I treasure. "Thank you for remembering," she wrote. "Somehow Mark's life has made his death easier for us. He wasn't bitter, had no quarrel with God, and didn't feel sorry for himself. He seemed to see himself as one whom God had richly blessed. And so he was. And so are we all."

My prayer partner, Carol, lost a 14-year-old son before I knew her. Afterward she called every pastor in her small community, asking each one to announce Hal's death on Sunday from their pulpits. And she asked them to convey this message to the people: "Nothing we gave Hal—an education, material things, even love—nothing counted except that he knew Jesus and has eternal life."

When a child is lost in death, it helps to remember that God is our partner in grief. Jesus has already gone through His sufferings and death and waits to minister to our pain.

When Death Is Imminent

We must ask God for keen discernment to know if He is going to heal a chronically ill person or if death is imminent. The apostle Peter once wrote, "I know that I will soon put (my body) aside as our Lord Jesus Christ has made clear to me" (2 Peter 1:14).

In our culture we seldom talk to the terminally ill about death—particularly children. But if we know death is near, do we do the patient an injustice by not addressing the issue?

Cancer, AIDS and other diseases are worldwide problems. We cannot piously assume that every chronically or acutely ill child or adult is going to be healed. Yes, of course we pray for healing. But we also try to lead our children to the Lord if they aren't saved. In God's economy, salvation takes priority over healing.

My prayer partner, Fran, is a nurse and physical therapist who has worked with many dying patients. Her 29-year-old son, Mark, came to the brink of death with advanced Hodgkin's disease some years ago. Fran knows firsthand what it is to face losing a child.

"We should remind our children that each of us will face physical death sometime," she told me, recalling her agonizing time of relinquishing Mark to God for His purposes to be worked out. "We're not promised we will be here when Jesus comes. I decided I had to prepare Mark for death or for healing. We are very grateful he was healed."

From her experience of dealing with the dying, Fran says as Christians we should do two things. First, make sure the patient has accepted Jesus as his Savior. Second, stop pretending that the person is not dying.

"Instead, help him deal with the fear of death that's common to all," she told me. "You can do this by praying for peace and assurance that to be absent from the body is to be present with the Lord (see 2 Corinthians 5:8). We must be loving, gentle and sensitive to the Holy Spirit in what we say."

She advises talking to your child about his eternal being—that he is a spirit, he has a soul, and he lives in a body. The spirit within him will live on through eternity—with the Lord if he knows Him; in dark despair if he doesn't.

Fran gives an illustration which she found helpful in talking to one dying friend. She suggests the mother of a young child could adapt it this way:

"Remember when we sent Grandma a special gift last year? We selected it, bought it, then sealed it with tape for mailing. On the package, I wrote our return address, then Grandma's address. We took it to the post office, paid the postage and gave it to the postmaster. He stamped it and put it aside to be shipped to Grandma.

"You are like that special package. Jesus bought you by giving His life for you. He sealed you with the Holy Spirit. Like the package waiting in the post office, you are waiting to be sent to our Father in heaven. We don't know when He'll send for you, but eventually an angel will deliver you to Him.

"We'll be separated for awhile, but Daddy and I will be along shortly, because Jesus also has bought us and is preparing us for sending to the Father. Remember your friend who died? You'll see him and others you know. But the One you will know best is Jesus.

"Jesus left heaven, came down to earth to live, and then died for us so we could be forgiven and made as pure as He is. He went back to heaven to prepare a wonderful place for you and for me, and for all those who love Him.

"I'm going to sit here and hold your hand until Jesus sends for you. Then I'll place your hand in His, and He will take you to be with Him."

Fran says it's a mistake to allow our children to think this earthly life is all there is. We must teach them about heaven, and that living on earth is only the tiniest slice of life in preparation for life in heaven.

Many times, mothers have not led their little children to Jesus, thinking they were too young or that there was plenty of time later. It's never too early, or too late, for you to do this. We should talk to our children about accepting Jesus even when they are small. Corrie ten Boom's mother helped her accept Jesus when she was five, and Corrie always remembered the exact moment.

We may be led to ask our dying children questions concerning forgiveness: "Is there anybody who's hurt you or that you are mad at? Let's pray and ask the Lord Jesus to help you forgive them. Then we'll thank Him for His forgiveness." Fran says this often is an important first step to take when preparing a child for death.

She also emphasizes that mothers should read aloud Scriptures which assure their children that there is no pain or sorrow where they are going and that they will have a far better life in heaven than they did on earth.

Healing, Health and Heaven

Paul left us encouragement in Romans 14:8. "If we live, we live to the Lord; and if we die, we die to the Lord. So, whether we live or die, we belong to the Lord."

That verse has a special meaning to me, because it was my Mom's favorite as I helped her through 13 months of agony before her death. I nursed her in the daytime and, at night, slept on a cot beside her bed. Besides talking a lot about our Savior, our favorite topics to discuss were healing, health and heaven. They were wonderful times spent searching the Scriptures for what God had to say on those three subjects.

I have clear memories of her final days when I read the Word aloud to her every morning. Although she couldn't respond, I knew in my spirit she was being comforted. Once she roused from a coma to shout three times, "Hallelujah! Hallelujah! Hallelujah!"

These were her last words, although she lingered three more weeks. I was beside her praying the Lord's Prayer when she died—an experience I'll forever cherish.

Scriptures to Share with the Dying

Here are some helpful Scriptures to share with a loved one facing the end of life on earth:

Even though I walk through the valley of the shadow of death, I will fear no evil, for you are with me (Psalm 23:4).

So do not fear, for I am with you; do not be dismayed, for I am your God. I will strengthen you and help you; I will uphold you with my righteous right hand (Isaiah 41:10).

And surely I am with you always, to the very end of the age (Matthew 28:20).

If I rise on the wings of the dawn, if I settle on the far side of the sea, even there your hand will guide me, your right hand will hold me fast (Psalm 139:9,10).

Do not let your hearts be troubled. Trust in God; trust also in me. In my Father's house are many rooms; if it were not so, I would have told you. I am going there to prepare a place for you. And if I go and prepare a place for you, I will come back and take you to be with me that you also may be where I am. You know the way to the place where I am going (John 14:1-3).

And this is what he promised us—even eternal life (1 John 2:25).

See that you do not look down on one of these little ones. For I tell you that their angels in heaven always see the face of my Father in heaven (Matthew 18:10).

After the Lord Jesus had spoken to them, he was taken up into heaven and he sat at the right hand of God (Mark 16:19).

Prayer

Lord, I thank You for _____ , whose absence has left such a void in my life. How I miss this precious one. How I long to hold him/her close again. Lord, thank You that You love _____ more than I do. Thank You for the assurance I have that my loved one is right now with You and is without pain or sorrow. Help me deal with my loss, grief, anger and inability to cope at times. Teach me how to draw on Your love and strength. Send the Comforter to comfort me in my sadness. Help me in time to share encouragement with others who have gone through a similar loss. I ask this in Jesus' name. Amen.

Note

1. Quin Sherrer and Ruthanne Garlock, *A Woman's Guide to Spirit-Filled Living* (Ann Arbor: Servant Publications, 1996), p. 167.

PART III

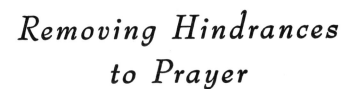

Removing Hindrances to Prayer

Chapter Ten

Dealing with Unforgiveness

"And when you stand praying, if you hold anything against anyone, forgive him, so that your Father in heaven may forgive you your sins."

MARK 11:25,26

Connie came home from work early one Tuesday afternoon to discover her high school son in bed with his girlfriend. "What do you mean?!" she screamed at the terrified girl. "You have no right to defile my home like this! Get out of my house!"

"Rob, I'll deal with you later. Get up and go mow that grass I told you to cut yesterday."

Fleeing to the bathroom, Connie sat on the edge of the tub, shaking and fighting to control her anger. How long had this been going on? How could she ever forgive Rob for stooping so low, especially in his own house? She was furious.

"Raising a teenager as a single parent is a lot more than I bargained for," she moaned. "Oh, God, help!"

Emma and Stuart are weary parents who have repeatedly forgiven their oldest son, but they have just about given up. A junkie, he has stolen almost everything of value from their home—money, a gun collection, sterling silver flatware and a stereo.

These hurting parents, like many others I've prayed with, are facing up to the deep wounds inflicted by their children. They know God requires them to forgive—yet they struggle. They ask the question many parents ask: How many times must I continue to forgive?

Of course it isn't easy, but as gently as I can, I remind them that unforgiveness is one of the greatest hindrances to prayer.

A Journey to Forgiveness

Gloria is a widow who experienced a most painful journey of forgiveness. Rarely have I met anyone whose countenance exuded such peace. Yet her life has been anything but peaceful. Her pilgrimage began late one night with a phone call from her married daughter, Lisa.

"Mom, can you come get the baby and me?" Lisa asked anxiously. "Randall just came in high and wild. I'm afraid he might do something crazy. I'd feel safer spending the night with you."

Gloria and her son, who'd just arrived home for his first military leave, drove across town. Upon arriving at her daughter's mobile home, they heard loud shouts and arguing. Her son jumped out of the car and raced to the front door. But before he got there, Randall opened fire. The bullet hit the young marine square in the chest, and he fell to the ground dead as his mother watched, horrified.

It's been some years now since the tragic loss of Gloria's son. A judicial technicality kept her son-in-law out of prison, but Lisa divorced him and asked Gloria to raise their baby. Life became more difficult when Lisa moved in with another man and had two more babies.

Gloria finally realized she could not continue dwelling on Randall's horrendous crime or her daughter's bad choices. Doing so would only keep her chained to her resentment. She began by telling the Lord her deepest, most painful feelings. Some she had never admitted before—ugly, angry ones. At that point, Gloria asked God to forgive her. Then, from her heart, she forgave her daughter and her son-in-law.

"My bitterness and resentment had infected our whole family," she said. "My daughter was mad at me; I was mad at her. I had to forgive and stop looking back. When I did, we began talking and laughing again. We could go on living. I enjoy raising my grandson and spending time with the other grandchildren. I pray for them every day and take them to church with me on Sundays. Now the future has hope."

God's grace had outstripped disappointment, prejudice and fear. Gloria chose to love and forgive her children—to a degree she never thought possible.

Forgiveness. Some people talk about it. Others, like Gloria, live it.

Love Makes Parents Vulnerable

Connie, Emma, Stuart, Gloria and millions of parents like them are vulnerable because they love their children.

Connie sought Christian counseling after the bedroom confrontation with Rob and his girlfriend. Shortly afterward, in prayer, she was able to release her hurt and forgive her son.

Emma and Stuart, despite many emotional struggles, continue to walk in forgiveness while praying their son will be delivered from drugs. There's no escaping the risk of being hurt as a parent, but forgiveness is always God's answer.

What is forgiveness? Forgiveness is an act of one's will. It's also a process that requires time for our emotions to come into agreement with the decision we have made. This takes longer for some than for others, but once we decide to take the first step toward forgiveness, we can depend on God's strength to help us continue the process.

The following elements are part of this process:

- Giving up the desire to punish or get even
- Excusing for a fault or offense
- Turning from defensiveness
- Ceasing to feel resentment

- Renouncing anger
- Absolving from payment

Jesus often warned His followers about the consequences of refusing to forgive. He told a story about a servant who owed the king an enormous debt—10,000 talents, or millions of dollars. When the servant begged for mercy, the king had great compassion and wiped away the debt. After he was forgiven, the servant met a man who owed him a very small amount. He demanded that the man pay every cent. When the king heard this, he called the servant, took back his forgiveness, and threw him into jail to be tortured until he could pay back all he owed (see Matthew 18:23-35).

Through this parable, Jesus paints a picture of our relationship to God:

1. God, our King, out of His great compassion, cancels our debts.
2. Like the servant, our sins (debts) against God are so enormous we can never repay them.
3. The sins which others commit against us are small and insignificant compared with our debt to our Master.
4. Our natural bent is to withhold forgiveness.
5. When we refuse to forgive others, we block God's flow of mercy and forgiveness to us.[1]

Like the unforgiving servant in Jesus' parable, we suffer torment whenever we refuse to forgive. Anyone who has wrestled with guilt understands this, for guilt is torment. God, through Christ's sacrificial death, has provided an answer: He forgives us.

Freedom from Bondage

Scripture makes it clear that unforgiveness keeps us in bondage to the devil. Paul wrote, "I have forgiven in the sight of Christ for your sake, in order that Satan might not outwit us. For we are not unaware of his schemes" (2 Corinthians 2:10,11).

Unforgivness a scheme of the devil? Yes, because Satan knows that if you harbor unforgiveness and bitterness in your heart, your prayers will be hindered. That is his goal.

Few of us decide intentionally to be unforgiving. So why do we hold on to our anger and desire for revenge? Frankly, because all of us are sinners. Adam and Eve's sin caused us to inherit a sinful nature—one driven to self-serving and rebellion against God.

On the Cross, Jesus took the punishment we deserved. His sacrificial death and triumph over the grave destroyed sin's power. Thus, when we repent and ask Him to forgive us, our sin account is marked, "Paid in full." But he requires that we now forgive our enemies.

That's a strong statement. Yet God's condition is indisputable: Forgiven by Him, we must forgive those who sin against us, just as Jesus did. He has not prescribed a legalistic duty; rather He's provided an opportunity for us to live fully guilt-free.

When we choose to forgive, we extend love and mercy to the one forgiven and release him from our judgment. This doesn't mean the person has no responsibility for his sin. But forgiveness cuts us free from bondage and opens the way for God to deal with him.

Paul tells us, "Be kind and compassionate to one another, forgiving each other, just as in Christ God forgave you" (Ephesians 4:32). The word "forgiving" in this verse means "to bestow a favor unconditionally."

Jesus clearly instructs us, "Forgive and you will be forgiven" (Luke 6:37). Here "forgive" means to "let loose from" or "to release, set at liberty."[2] Forgiveness is not a one-time choice. It is an ongoing process.

Forgiveness Started His Journey Back to God

One evening, shortly before my son, Keith, married, he and I sat on the side of his bed talking. He asked me, "Mom, do you know what triggered my return to the Lord? It's something you can share with other mothers."

"What?" I asked, my curiosity aroused.

"Things began to turn around the night I called you and Dad and asked you to forgive me," he said.

I remembered. He had dialed us from a pay phone outside the hotel conference room where he was enrolled in a success seminar. He had talked to me first, then to his dad. Each of us responded with the same words, "Keith, I forgive you."

"Even the secular world knows the necessity of forgiveness," Keith said, as we continued our talk. "In the seminar, they told us forgiveness is one way to prevent stress or sickness. Of course, they didn't tell us about the peace only Jesus can give—because they didn't know about that."

God had used a secular seminar to help Keith identify his need to ask our forgiveness.

As we talked, I thought back to a night long ago when I had made the choice to forgive my dad for abandoning our family when I was young. The pastor who was encouraging me to examine my own heart that night said, "Your father is responsible for his own wrongdoing. You must release your anger and ask God's forgiveness for any hidden bitterness if you want to receive His peace and blessing. Don't forget a biblical principle: What we sow, we reap," he added.

How much easier it was for me to forgive my son after having loosed my dad from my judgment years earlier. Just think, when I forgave Keith, I also set him free.

Stirring Up Anger

Fourteen-year-old Andy was practicing his chords on the piano when his father stuck his head into the living room and said, "Andy, is that all you know?"

To the dad's untrained ear, it sounded as if his son had been playing the same song for hours. Andy immediately stopped and never again played the piano for his dad.

Years later, in his twenties, Andy confessed to his dad that he'd resented him from that day on, misinterpreting his words to mean he didn't accept him or his music. The budding musician, crushed by his father's words, had harbored his hurt for years.

Pray that God will enable you to impart wisdom to your children. But ask Him to help you do it with kindness.

Thankfully, Andy's father, Pastor Charles Stanley, realized there was a wall in their relationship. At his initiation, they patiently worked through their need for forgiveness.[3]

"A harsh word stirs up anger," the writer of Proverbs reminds us (15:1). We can cut our children down when we angrily rebuke them or speak in other thoughtless, sarcastic ways. Unless forgiveness brings healing, we suffer the consequences of a broken relationship.

Scripture provides us with an excellent example in the virtuous wife. "She opens her mouth with wisdom, and on her tongue is the law of kindness" (Proverbs 31:26, *NKJV*). We can pray that God will enable us to impart wisdom to our children. But ask Him to help us do it with kindness.

How to Forgive: Humble Yourself

God's requirement to restore a broken relationship is simple: "Humble yourself." Not an easy task. Scripture says, "Clothe yourselves with humility toward one another, because, 'God opposes the proud but gives grace to the humble.' Humble yourselves, therefore, under God's mighty hand, that he may lift you up in due time" (1 Peter 5:5,6).

Most of us are afraid to let down our guard in front of our children. What if they see us as we really are? We could risk losing our place of authority in their lives. The fact is, when we ask their forgiveness, we're projecting true authority and strength. Such an act of humility can enhance our children's view of us.

When we are wrong, we can simply say, "I shouldn't have said that. You've been hurt by my words. Please forgive me. I'm sorry." Or we may need to add, "Is there something I can do to help straighten out this misunderstanding?"

Genuine humility will often encourage the child to ask your forgiveness for his or her behavior, and you can then discuss the entire episode without inflammatory, hurtful words.

One transparent mother of five told me, "When you see your own flesh—your sons and daughters—do things you've fought in yourself all your life, you know we're all sinners. Nobody is good but God. My oldest daughter did all the things 'good girls' don't do—but the truth is, if I'd had the courage as a youngster, I'd probably have done the same things. How could I not forgive my children?"

Right Timing and Right Attitude

When we know our words or actions have hurt our children, we need to do something about it as soon as the opportunity seems right. However, it's crucial to pray for the right timing, the right words and the right motive and attitude for ourselves and our children. Here is a suggested model for such a prayer:

> Father, I ask You to prepare my child to receive my apology. Help me speak honestly from my heart. I trust You to prepare the way and create the opportunity for this ministry of forgiveness to take place. Thank You, Lord, that You will give victory in this situation. Thank You for Your forgiveness, in Jesus' name. Amen.

'The grandest expression of love is to forgive," says Christian psychologist Richard P. Walters. "It is our most unselfish act and, therefore, the most difficult and rewarding."[4] Our act of forgiveness, like Jesus' act of love on the Cross, will have a profound impact on the child we forgive. We make the choice.

It is critically important to remember that forgiveness is often a progressive thing, a way of life we must nurture. Many hurts and resentments have been buried for years. Once we have opened ourselves to the forgiveness process, we must allow time for the Holy Spirit to change us and renew our thoughts.

Accepting Forgiveness

Christian parents who cannot or will not forgive themselves will struggle to forgive their children. When we refuse to forgive ourselves, we are saying, *Jesus' sacrifice is not sufficient for me.*

Take Claudia, for example, a mother who wrestled with her own sense of failure. "I've told the Lord dozens of times that I've forgiven my son for robbing a convenience store and going to prison. But the ugly words I shouted at Bob when I was mad—words like 'stupid' and 'disgraceful'—still ring in my ears night and day," she told me as I prayed with her after a ladies' meeting.

Claudia had written Bob in prison and asked his forgiveness, and he'd written back, assuring her he wanted their relationship restored. Still, she had no peace.

"If you and Bob have forgiven each other, then God forgives you both," I assured her. "Just accept His forgiveness. You see, the enemy wants to torment you with guilt; but you must believe what God says, not what the enemy says. Believe the truth."

For her that was the enabling key. After we talked, she prayed again, accepted God's gift of forgiveness, and left with a gleam of victory in her eye.

The "Ding-Dong" Principle

I told Claudia a story that has helped me whenever I struggle with unforgiveness and self-condemnation. The renowned Dutch evangelist, Corrie ten Boom, gave this illustration:

Up in that church tower is a bell which is rung by pulling on a rope. After the sexton lets go of the rope, the bell keeps on swinging. First ding, then dong. Slower and slower until there's a final dong and it stops. When we forgive someone, we take our hands off the rope. But if we've been tugging at our grievances for a long time, we mustn't be surprised when the old angry thoughts keep coming for awhile. They're just the ding-dongs of the old bell slowing down.[5]

Though God forgets, we humans tend to remember our old sins. These are the ding-dongs of our past. How badly we need to stop "preserving the evidence" in our memory banks and focus on God's promise: "If we confess our sins, he is faithful and just and will forgive us our sins and purify us from all unrighteousness" (1 John 1:9).

God's forgiveness is a free gift, yet thousands of Christians have not yet accepted this special gift for themselves. The Lord said, "I have swept away your offenses like a cloud, your sins like the morning mist" (Isaiah 44:22).

Forgiveness, like love, is a risk. Yet in faith and by our choice, we offer it whether our children forgive us or not. That's a risk God asks us to take. And if we want our prayers answered, we have no other choice.

As Corrie ten Boom often said, "Saints, take your hands off the rope—let go. Let God."

Prayer

Lord, forgive me for not believing the blood of Jesus is sufficient to cover my sins. I accept Your forgiveness, and I choose to forgive myself. I refuse to listen to the lies of the accuser any longer. Heavenly Father, I believe Your Word that says my offenses are wiped away like a heavy mist, buried in the sea of forgetfulness, forgiven and forgotten by You.

Thank You for such reassurance. I praise You for allowing Jesus to die for me. What an all-sufficient, all-encompassing Father You are to me! I praise You for allowing Jesus to die for me. Amen.

Prayer

Thank You, Father, for sending Jesus as an atonement for my sins. Thank You for forgiving me and enabling me to forgive those who wrong me. Help me to be willing to continually forgive my children—and all others who hurt me.

Lord, help me speak pleasant, encouraging words to my children; help me to bless them and not to curse them through my careless words. Show me how to humble myself and make amends. I ask in Jesus' name, amen.

Notes

1. JoAnne Sekowsky, *Forgiveness: A Two-Way Street* (Lynnwood, Wash.: Aglow Publications, 1985), p. 4.
2. W.E. Vine, *An Expository Dictionary of New Testament Words* (Grand Rapids: Fleming Revell, 1966), p. 463.
3. Charles Stanley, *Forgiveness* (Nashville: Thomas Nelson, 1987), pp. 21, 22.
4. Dr. Richard P. Walters, *Anger—Yours and Mine and What to Do About It* (Grand Rapids: Zondervan, 1981), p. 82.
5. Corrie ten Boom, *Tramp for the Lord* (Grand Rapids: Fleming Revell, 1974), pp. 179, 180.

Chapter Eleven

Overcoming Disappointment and Anger

In your anger do not sin. Do not let the
sun go down while you are still angry,
and do not give the devil a foothold.
EPHESIANS 4:26,27

"Wait until that kid gets home! I'll tear him up," the enraged father shouted as he paced the floor at three in the morning. "If I lose any more sleep, I won't get to work on time. It's not unreasonable to expect a 16-year-old to be in at midnight!"

"But what if something awful has happened to him, like a car wreck?" his wife sobbed as she poured the last of the coffee. "You've got to have mercy, Daniel, and consider why Ted is over three hours late coming home...."

Can you identify with this angry father and worried mom? Have you ever vacillated between anger and anxiety because your child wasn't home by curfew? As a mother who survived three in their teens at the same time, I can relate. Sometimes I was convinced my children never knew that Alexander Graham Bell had invented the telephone!

Why do so many of us fail in handling everyday situations with our children? I see at least two reasons: (1) We tend to react out of our own suspicions and hurts; (2) Seldom do we ask the Lord for wisdom to handle our reactions or the child's discipline following an infraction of household rules.

I Know She Can Do Better

Parents' expectations for their child's academic achievement affect the way the parents react at report card time. Once when my husband was in the hospital, I asked his nurse about her family.

"My daughter brought home a C on her report card last night, so I've decided not to have a birthday party for her this weekend when she turns eight," she related.

"Is that really fair?" I asked, watching her adjust the IV tube. "Do you want her to always remember that Mom cancelled her eighth birthday party because of a math grade? Can't you find some other way to discipline or to help her improve? I still remember punishment I received on my birthday as a child and how wounded I was."

"I never thought about my reaction as wounding her," she replied, looking surprised. "I only thought about my own disappointment, because I know she can do better in math."

"If you don't mind my saying so, I think you may need to forgive your little girl for disappointing you," I said carefully. "You could set her free by forgiving her."

"Really?!" she exclaimed, looking at me intently. I had obviously gotten her attention. She quietly gathered up her equipment to leave the room, thinking over what I'd said.

"I guess I do need to forgive her," she agreed. "I'll go ahead with her birthday party and find some other way to deal with the math problem."

While having a child make a C in math seems trivial to some, many parents withhold much more than a birthday party from a youngster who brings home less than straight A's. Why is that? The parents know their child has the potential to do better, that's true. But more than likely, the real problem lies with parental pride that's offended when children do less than their best. We need to examine our motives when we put such high demands on our children.

Unconditional Love

Parents want the best for their children, and it's not surprising that their expectations are high. But how do they react when their high hopes turn to disappointments? For Christians, there is one answer: They should respond with unconditional love, difficult though it may be. Through prayer, the Lord can help you guide your child in reaching his or her full potential, without applying undue pressure.

When Jeanne moved with her husband to Asia, she prayed for healing of the rift with her teenage daughter, Deb, who was staying behind to attend college. On more than one occasion during her stormy high school years, Deb had screamed, "I hate what you stand for, Mom! You're a hypocrite! How can you say you're a Christian when you yell at me so much?"

A few months into Deb's first year in college, she called her mother from the States. "Mom, I'm expecting a baby."

Deb was dumbfounded when she heard her mother shriek with excitement, "Oh, I'm going to be a grandmother!" At that moment, it didn't occur to Jeanne to scold her daughter.

Her next words surprised Deb even more. "Darling, I can't wait to meet Gary. I'll fly right home and give you the kind of wedding you've always dreamed of."

"You will?" Deb asked incredulously. "Mom, you mean you aren't going to scream and yell at me? You will come meet Gary and give me a wedding? Wow, I can't believe this is my mom." A few days later, Jeanne was in Oklahoma with Deb, helping with wedding plans. After spending a day with her future son-in-law, Jeanne welcomed him into the family.

I asked Jeanne how she was able to respond so positively to

Deb's situation of being pregnant out of wedlock. "After leaving the States, I did a lot of soul-searching about my poor example to my daughter," she replied. "I realized that if she couldn't see Christ's love in my life, I had failed God. I asked Him to cleanse my heart and change my ways."

"What about forgiving Deb?" I asked.

"I had forgiven Deb of all the things she'd done to exasperate me, and my heart was overflowing with love for her when she called," Jeanne explained. "Remember, I'd prayed a long time before I could respond that way. All I could think about was, 'I'm going to be a grandmother!'—and I was excited about that prospect."

Jeanne and Deb talked through their hurts, forgave each other, and established a close mother-daughter relationship. Today Jeanne is delighted with her two grandchildren.

Don't React—Respond

It's hard not to react negatively—speaking words we later wish we'd swallowed—when we see our children heading in a direction we know is wrong. Many parents today are faced with the decision of how to react to a variety of distressing situations:

- A child withdrawing from life because of rejection
- A single daughter using contraceptives
- A son living with his girlfriend
- A child making close friends among peers who are negative influences
- A son or daughter following a homosexual lifestyle
- A child openly rebelling against Christian values taught at home
- A child in trouble with the law
- A child addicted to drugs or alcohol

To remain loving toward our children without implying approval of their questionable behavior is as difficult as walking a tightrope But this Scripture gives us good advice: "If anyone speaks, he should do it as one speaking the very words of God" (1 Peter 4:11).

One mother, faced with her daughter's elopement, told her, "Let's wait to discuss this until after I've absorbed the shock. This is hard for me. Please give me some thinking time."

Another mom, shaken by a son's decision, said, "Son, this is important to me, but it's hard for me to talk about it right now. Can we discuss it in the morning?"

Failure Is Not Final

Many parents pray for years for their children, wanting them to be all God created them to be. Then the parents watch helplessly when the children flounder or make foolish decisions.

Mary Rae Deatrick, in her book, *Easing the Pain of Parenthood*, has a word for parents in panic situations:

> Facing our emotions, facing facts and accepting the circumstances opens the door to our casting the burden on the Lord in prayer. We are now ready to receive from God our comfort, our emotional healing and our guidance....Let us correct what we can correct, change what we can change, and forgive all the mess that is left over. I beseech you not to think of failure as final.[1]

The Futility of Anger

Anger—intense anger Dolores didn't know she was capable of harboring—boiled to the point of explosion one day. She discovered her 13-year-old Willie smoking marijuana with his friends in the woods behind their house. She grabbed him by the ear, jerked him up and propelled him along the path toward home. "Why are you doing this to me?" she yelled, shaking with rage. He didn't bother to answer.

Alarmed by her unbridled anger toward her son, Dolores dug through Scripture until she found something to help bring her anger under control. A verse in James became her lifeline: "Be quick to listen, slow to speak and slow to become angry, for man's anger does not bring about the righteous life that God desires" (James 1:19,20).

"I realized anger was a useless indulgence," she said. "My job was to love Willie and to try to keep communication open with him. Every time I'd get angry, I'd pray, 'Lord, I know my anger will not make a righteous man out of my son. Only Your power can do that.'"

Willie got an after-school job, then bought a big, black motorcycle. Many nights he stayed out long past curfew. Dolores would wake up in a cold sweat, imagining his bloody body entangled in wreckage in some roadside ditch. Days passed when she wondered if there was any hope at all for Willie.

"I finally confessed that I was a poor mother, and I asked Jesus to forgive me," she told me. "That was primary to forgiving Willie for being such a difficult son. Even at that, I had to keep on forgiving him every single day."

For five long years, Dolores tried to communicate with Willie without seeing much improvement. During that time the Lord had given her an incredible idea: She made herself a "first-aid book" containing promises from the Bible. She would read this book over and over until a tiny spark of hope was kindled in her heart. God's promises were all she had to cling to when she knew Willie was still smoking marijuana behind her back.

Forgiveness Began a New Work

Dolores and her husband made a significant decision—to pull back from Willie and not reach out to him, to wait for him to come to them. But they never stopped praying for him.

One spring afternoon, just after his twentieth birthday, Willie came home and fell on his mother's shoulder, crying for no apparent reason. She and her husband held Willie while he sobbed his heart out. "I've been feeling lonely and abandoned lately, Mom," he confessed. "I don't like living like this." Forgiveness began a new work in all their hearts, but old hurts and past mistakes had to be dealt with.

> *"My confidence was in God. His kindness brought my son to repentance."*

"Little by little, Satan's work of planting lies in Willie's mind was uncovered," she told me. "His dad and I prayed for him to be set free, and we talked honestly with him about our mistakes and disappointments. When the time was right, we talked with him about God.

There was no instant cure for Willie. His deliverance from marijuana, alcohol and chewing tobacco was gradual. For nine years his parents had been on a rollercoaster with him—praying, forgiving, praying, forgiving and praying some more. But after he made a commitment to the Lord, Willie became a joy to his parents. He even got involved in a part-time prison ministry.

"My confidence was in God Himself," Dolores said. "His kindness brought my son to repentance."

Approach the Throne of Grace

We can relinquish all our hurt, pain and disappointment to Jesus, our great high priest. Wallowing in our failures is a dead-end road. Instead, let the Lord minister fresh grace and encouragement to you through these comforting words:

> For we do not have a high priest who is unable to sympathize with our weaknesses, but we have one who has been tempted in every way, just as we are—yet was without sin. Let us then approach the throne of grace with

confidence, so that we may receive mercy and find grace to help us in our time of need (Hebrews 4:15,16).

Grace will help in our time of need. It's God's enablement to help us respond in love to our children. Grace—ask Him for it!

When Your Child Disappoints You

Children are bound to disappoint you. It goes with the territory, a basic fact of parenting. Inevitably, parents have hopes and expectations for their children—high hopes that they will marry "well," choose the "right" career, live their lives according to "good" standards. When parents' fantasies don't materialize, they feel let down—in a word, disappointed.

My friends Hanna and Bill were disappointed in their son Curtis, who hadn't had a job in a year. They were driving to their Florida vacation cottage, discussing the problem when Hanna said, "Honey, maybe our expectations for Curtis are too high—maybe we want him to excel because of our own pride. He likes to work with his hands. He's not suited to working at a bank or an office the way you are."

"I think you're right," Bill answered, nodding his head. "I've thought about this a lot over the past year. Let's relinquish this to the Lord."

Right there in the car, they prayed aloud and released Curtis to the Lord, asking God to work His will in their son. The next week, he got a job working outdoors with his hands. Hanna told me about it later as we sat on the porch of their vacation cottage, watching her husband and son fish in the bay.

"We decided we couldn't play God in Curtis's life anymore," she said. "We were concerned about his financial situation. While he was off work that year, he built a log home for his family, but he needed an income. When we took our hands off the situation, in a sense we forgave him for disappointing us. Then God provided the job he needed. Now Bill and I both have a wonderful relationship with our son."

Dr. James Dobson encourages us with this advice:

> It is simply not prudent to write off a son or daughter, no matter how foolish, irritating, selfish or insane a child may seem to be. You need to be there, not only while their canoe is bouncing precariously, but after the river runs smooth again. You have the remainder of your life to reconstruct the relationship that is now in jeopardy. Don't let anger fester for too long. Make the first move toward reconciliation.[2]

Parents' dreams and goals for their children often diminish or are obliterated by life's obstacles or wrong choices. They can easily become disappointed and must find a way to adjust.

Forgiveness: An Oft-Repeated Necessity

Debbie wrote about her experience. "I'm not sure when my children's misbehavior stopped being a normal part of childhood that required correction, and started being a catalyst for my temper," she wrote. "My kids did so many things that angered me: Jim's arguing, Jerry's tattling, Julie's emotional outbursts, Janet's whining."

At first, Debbie dismissed her flare-ups as a temporary result of cranky kids. Later, she faced the fact that she dreaded their arrival home from school. When she prayed about it, the Lord showed her she had never forgiven her children.

"How had I missed the obvious?" she asked. "Though I'd asked God to forgive me, I hadn't sought help in forgiving my children's insults. No wonder the first offense of the morning made me mad. I wanted to get rid of my children's yesterdays, so I gave God the arguing, tattling, outbursts and whining. I asked Him to help me forgive as He does—with nothing left clinging. But immediately I thought, *I'm going to have to do this a thousand times before my kids are grown!*"[3]

Why Have You
Treated Us Like This?

Does it offer you any comfort to know that Jesus' mother was anxious about Him? Maybe even disappointed? Remember when He was 12 years old and the family was returning home after spending some days at the Feast of Passover in Jerusalem? They assumed He was in their caravan, but when they began looking for Him among their acquaintances, He was missing. Returning to Jerusalem, they began an all-out search.

They found Him in the Temple, of all places, sitting among the teachers, asking questions and listening. Mary had a question for Him—one which mothers have asked through the centuries. "Son, why have you treated us like this?" (Luke 2:48).

How many of us have lain awake into the wee hours of the morning, waiting for our children to come home?

Unique Individuals

Many parents have difficulty recognizing their children as unique gifts from God. We tend to want to mold them into careers we like or see them marry to "better themselves," or we push them to fulfill dreams we once dreamed for ourselves. The Bible, however, tells us each child has an individual bent or talent:

> Train up a child in the way he should go [and in keeping with his individual gift or bent], and when he is old he will not depart from it (Proverbs 22:6, *Amp.*).

God has a plan and pattern for every one of us, including our children. Our role as Christian parents necessitates relinquishing them, so they might find God's will for their lives and see His purposes fulfilled in them.

How to Love This Son?

When Sue discovered her son had given his younger sister drugs, she was horrified. "I wanted to pack his bags, throw him out and padlock the front door," she told me. "I felt he'd undermined our family, making a mockery of everything we'd taught and lived. I lost all the trust and respect I had for him."

Her husband, Gene, brought her back on course. "When God gave us our children, we didn't put in an order for what we wanted. These are what we got," he reminded her. "Make up your mind that they are our children and we're supposed to love them, no matter what. Our son needs us now."

Sue realized her husband was right. Being disappointed doesn't mean we quit loving our children. It means we have an even greater opportunity to trust for God's love and forgiveness.

The Anguish of Suicide

Thousands of parents suffer the trauma of losing a child to suicide, causing them not only to grieve the loss of a child, but to struggle with guilt, shame, anger and other raw emotions which surface.

Nina has been through this experience. Her 28-year-old son, Bud, the father of two children, hanged himself one Monday morning after a quarrel with his wife. She had been out all night working as a barmaid—a job he didn't want her to have. She insisted on keeping it because the tips were good and the family had financial problems.

Months after the tragedy, Nina talked to her Sunday School teacher about the frustration and anger she felt.

"Could it be that you have unforgiveness toward God for disappointing you?" the teacher asked. "Or toward your son because he chose this way of dealing with his problems?"

"I'm not aware of it," Nina responded. "But if you sense that, maybe I need to forgive both of them."

Cleansing tears—long overdue tears—began pouring down

her face. "God, forgive me for holding unforgiveness toward my son for doing this. God, I forgive Bud," she prayed. "And Lord, I'm sorry I blamed You for his death. Please forgive me." More tears fell, and a warm, welcome peace enveloped her.

"Satan is the one who comes to steal, kill and destroy. I know that now. It wasn't God who killed my son," she shared with me. "It's amazing that I was unaware of the bitterness and unforgiveness I was harboring until my teacher talked to me," she said.

"I felt such release after forgiving, and it was a starting point that drew me closer to the Lord. Eventually my husband and daughter were drawn to Him, too. Now all of us are committed to Jesus Christ; we're not just Sunday pew-sitters."

I have found the best way to deal with my anger is not to let grievances accumulate. Then I can leave disappointments and high expectations for my children with God—in prayer.

Prayer

Lord, I admit there are times when I'm so disappointed in my child that I can't see anything good or positive in him/her. Forgive me for looking only at the imperfections, forgetting that I need to trust You, who does everything in the right way and at the right time. Lord, only You know the deepest needs of my child's heart; only You know when _____'s particular situation is fully ripe for Your answer. Help me to take times of disappointment and heartache and make them times of learning and training for future usefulness. I commit _____ into Your hands, Father, and I thank You that victory is on the way for this child. In Jesus' name I pray, with thanksgiving for all Your blessings. Amen.

Prayer

Father, thank You for Your unlimited grace. I now ask You to help me receive it, so that I can respond to my children with Jesus' love and acceptance. In His name, amen.

Notes

1. Mary Rae Deatrick, *Easing the Pain of Parenthood* (Portland, Oreg.: Harvest House, 1979), p. 40.
2. Dr. James Dobson, *Parenting Isn't for Cowards* (Dallas: Word Books, 1987), p. 55.
3. Debbie Hedstrom, "A Mom's Secret Weapon: Forgiveness," *Aglow* (December 1987).

Chapter Twelve

Surrendering Your Guilt, Fear and Pride

For God has not given us a spirit of fear,
but of power and of love and of a sound mind.
2 TIMOTHY 1:7, *NKJV*

Three major weapons the enemy uses against us to hinder our prayer efforts are guilt, fear and pride. We may feel guilty that we didn't do a better job of parenting. Or fearful our mistakes will keep our children from reaching God's full potential. Or nurse our wounded pride because our children have dreadfully disappointed us.

Have you ever felt that what you did for your children was too little and too late? Then you are guilt-ridden with "if only" scenarios. If only you had prayed sooner, taught earlier, loved more, communicated better—perhaps such-and-such wouldn't have happened. "If only" is a dead-end street to hopelessness.

None of us is a perfect parent. Only God can claim that title. But He is a God who loves us and redeems our mistakes when we cooperate with Him. Though we can't change the past, we can trust God to help us make amends and move into the future with hope—not fear.

Many of the things we fear will never happen anyway. And the troubles which do come our way usually turn out not to be so fearsome as we'd thought. God gives grace to enable us to walk through the present. We must avoid letting our imaginations run wild with worrying over what might happen on the road ahead.

"Worry means 'to divide into parts,'" says one Bible commentator. "[It] suggests a distraction, a preoccupation with things causing anxiety, stress and pressure. Jesus speaks against worry and anxiety because of the watchful care of a heavenly Father who is ever mindful of our daily needs."[1]

Seeing Our Children as God Sees Them

One mother told me how upset she was once when—despite her prayers—her son suffered a great disappointment. The college of his choice rejected him, and he was very angry. She knew the blow came because of his lack of diligence in his studies. But still, it was painful. As she wept and prayed, the Lord spoke gently to her spirit, saying, "He was mine before he was yours—and I love him more than you do. I won't hurt him any more than I have to."

The guilt, worry and fear left her as she saw the situation from God's perspective, and knew He was applying gentle discipline. A few months later, another college offered him a scholarship, and it turned out to be a wonderful door of opportunity. Yes, we can trust a loving heavenly Father to work out the difficulties in our children's lives.

Every child of His, every born-again believer, has promises from the heavenly Father on which to base his life. When we read through the Bible, we find many promises applying to our individual family's difficulty. Only God knows when a particular situation is fully ripe for His answer. While we wait with faith and patience to inherit those promises, we can be reassured by these faith-building verses:

He who has begun a good work in you will complete it until the day of Jesus Christ (Philippians 1:6, *NKJV*).

Now faith is being sure of what we hope for and certain of what we do not see (Hebrews 11:1).

I know whom I have believed, and am convinced that he is able to guard what I have entrusted to him for that day (2 Timothy 1:12).

I am the Lord, the God of all mankind. Is anything too hard for me? (Jeremiah 32:27).

Arise, cry out in the night...pour out your heart like water in the presence of the Lord. Lift up your hands to him for the lives of your children (Lamentations 2:19).

Would He Ever Change?

One mother battled with fear about her son until, one day, the Lord spoke to her as she walked on the beach. She shared her story with me:

When my son Mike turned sixteen, it seemed I'd lost touch with him. He was uptight and silent a lot. Simply in a shell. Worst of all, there was evidence he'd cut himself off from God, too. I watched powerlessly as other boys exerted more influence over him than we did at home. My only recourse was prayer.

Then late one afternoon, I was walking the beach alone, talking to the Lord about Mike. After more than an hour, I reached down and picked up a small brown-and-white shell that was being tossed about helplessly by the waves. When I did, I had an inner awareness that God was saying, "Leave your fear here on the beach. Think about this shell—it had much potential for growth. So does your son. Just trust Me to polish and perfect him."

Sally took her "promise shell" home, washed it in bleach, and set it on the kitchen window ledge. Often she'd pick it up and, holding it high in the air, breathe a triumphant reminder, "Lord, You promised."

Mike drifted further and further into open rebellion. One afternoon, he stormed out of the house screaming at his mother, "I can't be the kind of Christian you want me to be!" then disappeared until the wee hours of the morning.

Months crept by and he continued to get into all kinds of teenage mischief. Sally continued her travailing prayer, while fighting hard not to let fear envelop her with "What if this happens to him...?"

Mike went away to college. Still there was no sign of repentance or change for the better. Four years after God gave Sally that promise on the beach, she felt an urgency to write to her son about her special "promise shell." She ended her letter with a paraphrase of the Scripture she'd clung to: "I've held unswervingly to the hope I profess, for He who promised is faithful" (see Hebrews 10:23).

Mike wrote back, "Mom, your letter made me so happy I almost cried. You don't know this, but Tuesday—the night you wrote the letter—I went into the city to hear a Christian band perform. I'd really been in the pit, but I gave it all to God. I feel great. I know it won't be easy, but we'll make it this time. I appreciate now all that you and Dad have done for me. Thanks. And thank God for His 'promise shell.'"

When you ask Him, God often will give you a special assurance for your children. It may come from a Scripture verse or, as in Sally's case, from something personal God whispers to your spirit. When it comes, you can stand on that word with sure faith until you see His promise actually fulfilled. You will have some hours of persistent prayer in store, but you—we—must never give up. Nor must we give in to fear or guilt. God is faithful.

Dealing with Pride

Pride is a deadly foe—poison, actually—for a Christian. One of my friends often says, "Pride is spelled P-R-I-D-E with 'I' in the middle. Pride always centers on self." The writer of Proverbs warns, "When pride comes, then comes disgrace, but with humility comes wisdom" (Proverbs 11:2).

When Martha Jane learned her unmarried daughter, Gail, was pregnant, she felt her pride had been run over by a rock crusher. "No one can understand how much the mother is hurt and humiliated," she admitted.

> *"I finally laid down all my pride and became a loving buffer for my daughter."*

"One moment you want to hold your daughter and weep, 'Poor baby!' The next moment, you cry, 'How could she do this to me? What will our relatives say? What will our friends say?'

"I finally laid down all my pride and became a loving buffer for my daughter—protecting her from the outside world. Gail enrolled in a school for unwed mothers and decided she would keep her baby. After her son was born, I took a leave of absence from teaching and stayed home with the baby so Gail could finish high school."

Martha Jane looks back on it as one of her most rewarding years. She propped up her Bible and read it aloud as she fed or rocked the baby. She memorized up to 25 chapters of Scripture—nourishing her own soul as she nourished her first grandchild with love. Hugging him close to her bosom and reading God's Word aloud, she began believing in her heart who she is in Jesus, that His promises in the Word are for her and her family. She also spent a lot of time praying—for her daughter, the baby and her own family.

The new grandbaby also affected her husband's life. He had been having affairs for years. After the baby arrived, he stopped running around and their family drew closer together. Two years later, after the baby's father conquered his drug problem, Gail married him and they established a Christian home.

But Martha Jane wasn't the only one who had to deal with her pride. Her teenage son was embarrassed when his sister became pregnant. At first he went into denial about it. But right after the baby was born, he went to see him in the hospital. One peek and he came away with acceptance. And Martha Jane believes he forgave Gail at the same time.

Parents and siblings who have dealt with pregnant-out-of-wedlock children tell me they first must deal with their own sense of failure, shame and guilt, then with anger toward others for not understanding. They had to forgive the children involved, but that was only part of their battle. They also struggled with unforgiveness toward themselves and/or others who did not empathize with the crisis in their family.

A Painful Mother's Day Memory

"I always pushed aside the idea that my daughter might get pregnant before she married," Grace shared with me. "She did get pregnant, but she decided to get an abortion. I pleaded with her not to do it, but she insisted. To keep her from going to some back-alley shop, I went with her to a clinic that was open on Sundays. She had her abortion on Mother's Day."

Grace said dealing with the trauma of her daughter's decision to get an abortion was more difficult than learning that the girl was pregnant. "But as a Christian mother, I could not withhold love and forgiveness," she told me. "I forgave my daughter, even though I had been strongly opposed to her decision. I asked God to forgive her, then I asked for forgiveness for my part in it.

"My daughter is 30 now, married but childless. Every year on Mother's Day she gets sick over the memory of her sin. I've told her that her sin is covered by the blood of Jesus because she confessed and asked for forgiveness. Now she needs to forgive herself and receive God's healing."

Here is a mother who is an example to all of us who may have harshly judged a daughter, a relative or a friend's daughter for having an abortion. Their pain is excruciating when they realize the significance of their decision. God, help us not to increase that pain by rejecting them!

The Scripture teaches that when an individual sins, those who are spiritual "should restore him gently" (Galatians 6:1).

Another mother shared with me her grief over her own participation in her daughter's sin. "My daughter has had three abortions, and I helped her get the first one," she said. "I really have had a hard time with my own guilt, let alone trying to forgive my daughter for killing two more of my grandbabies." She cried as we prayed, asking God to forgive and cleanse her of guilt and pride—and then to help her forgive and restore her daughter.

The Most Excellent Way

It's a basic human tendency to feel shame when our children's behavior violates our value system, and to feel proud when their behavior pleases us.

A neat, obedient daughter is easier to accept and love than a son who is messy, disobedient and sassy. And a son who makes excellent grades and shows respect for his parents will be more readily favored than a daughter who runs with a bad crowd, breaks curfew and takes drugs.

How can we parents deal with this? Do we take great pride in one child and ignore the good qualities in another? Do we pray more for one than for another? Do we grit our teeth and overlook our children's faults or bad behavior? Do we deny our inclination to prefer one over another? Do we condemn ourselves for our feelings?

The apostle Paul comes to our rescue with a practical word: "I will show you the most excellent way" (1 Corinthians 12:31). That way, parents, is to love our children with God's love. To make an exchange: our limited human love for His inexhaustible divine love.

Recognize Uniqueness

"Recognizing the uniqueness of our children, their creative bent, is a key to avoiding the competitiveness that can develop between brothers and sisters," says Helen Hosier in her book, *You Never Stop Being a Parent.* "We can't always treat them alike—temperamental differences come into play, as well as physiological and emotional variations. No two personalities are going to be exactly alike."[2]

My friend Peggy has a unique relationship with her five children. "Each one thinks he or she is my favorite!" she told me with a grin. "I think every child in the world wants to think he is his mother's most beloved. I've always worked hard at spending quality time with each one of mine, so he or she feels special. Also, I've tried to be genuinely interested in their activities, whether it was art, music, interior design or tennis. Still, I have to say, God is the one who gives me creative ways to be the mother each of them needs."

As Peggy's experience illustrates, there are positive ways to take pride in our children and boost their self-esteem. Every child longs to know his parents are proud of him. But we must guard against trying to live our lives through our children by manipulating their choices of careers, friends or spouses. This attitude fosters a sinful pride and ultimately undermines the parent-child relationship.

Only the Holy Spirit can help us to lay aside these hindrances to prayer—guilt, fear and pride—so we can be effective intercessors for our children.

Prayer

Father, may we, like You, be perpetual forgivers. Help us to show our children what precious gifts they are to us. Equip us to be better parents. If any of our children perceive themselves as unworthy or unloved, let us become aware so we can help reassure them of our love.

Thank You, Lord, for loving us unconditionally and for helping us to do the same for our children. We speak blessings upon all our children, and we thank You for sending them as blessings to us. Amen.

Prayer

Father, I desire to have the kind of love that will drive out fear in my life. Help me walk in it every day—trusting that You have everything in my life under control, including my children's needs. I give You the guilt, pride and fear that hinders my prayers. In faith, I say again, I trust You, my loving heavenly Father. Thank You, in Jesus' name.

Scriptures to Meditate Upon

When I am afraid, I will trust in you.
In God, whose word I praise,
in God I trust; I will not be afraid.
What can mortal man do to me?
(Psalm 56:3,4)

Trust in the Lord with all your heart and
lean not on your own understanding;
in all your ways acknowledge him,
and he will make your paths straight.
(Proverbs 3:5,6)

Instead of your shame you shall have double honor,
And instead of confusion they shall
rejoice in their portion.
Therefore in their land they shall possess double;
Everlasting joy shall be theirs.
(Isaiah 61:7, *NKJV*)

Notes

1. *Spirit-Filled Life Bible* (Nashville: Thomas Nelson, 1991), footnote on p. 1415.
2. Helen Hosier, *You Never Stop Being a Parent* (Grand Rapids: Fleming Revell, 1986), p. 52.

PART IV

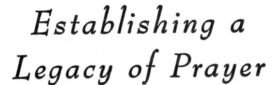

Establishing a
Legacy of Prayer

Chapter Thirteen

Imparting Blessings to Your Children

The Lord bless you and keep you; the Lord make his face shine upon you and be gracious to you; the Lord turn his face toward you and give you peace.

NUMBERS 6:24-26

How would you respond if your youngest daughter insisted on marrying a young man with a terrible temper, someone who had caused her grief, heartache and tears throughout the eight years of their relationship?

This was the crisis facing pastor Jamie Buckingham and his wife, Jackie, when Sandy, youngest of their five children, told them she was marrying Jerry. Jackie tells their story:

> We had given each of our older children the freedom to make their own choices, but we severely questioned Sandy's judgment when it came to Jerry, whom she had dated all the way through high school. In fact, we had done everything we could to break up their relationship.
>
> Although Jerry was a Christian and a member of our church, his early years had not been spent in a Christian home. His parents had accepted Christ about the time Jerry entered his teens, and afterward they were dedi-

cated to the Lord. But those earlier, violent years had scarred their son.

Jerry was an outstanding athlete, but was impulsive, short-tempered and often violent. At other times, he and Sandy had physically battered each other, sometimes in public. This was entirely foreign to our gentle way of life, and Jamie and I were deeply concerned Sandy might become an abused wife if she married Jerry.

We met with Jerry's parents. They were equally concerned. We recommended counseling for the kids, and they both submitted themselves to a friend who has a deliverance ministry. Things got better, but evidences of the old life hung on. His parents cooperated with us by insisting Sandy and Jerry break off their relationship for a year. Sandy went off to a college in the midwest, and Jerry went to school in a different state.

At the end of the year, Sandy was back home. The phone bills were staggering; and the relationship, even from afar, was just as strong. There was another year of separation when Jerry joined the U.S. Coast Guard. Jamie and I kept praying, hoping that Sandy would meet another boy; or Jerry, another girl.

Why Can't You See the Good?

"Mom," Sandy kept saying, "Why can't you see the good in Jerry that I see? Underneath that rough exterior is a real man of God. He's frightened of you and Dad. That's the reason he seems unfriendly when he's around you."

Then one day Sandy made her announcement. "Jerry and I are going to get married. We'll not do it until you and Dad bless us, but we are going to get married."

I talked with Jamie. "We've done everything we can to break them up," he said. "Maybe God wants us to start blessing them rather than cursing them."

We looked at Matthew 18:18 together: "I tell you the truth, whatever you bind on earth will be bound in heaven, and whatever you loose on earth will be loosed in heaven."

"Let's loose them," Jamie suggested.

"OK," I agreed warily.

Jerry was to be home the next week on leave from the Coast Guard. We took the young couple out to dinner, and Jamie laid it out for them to understand. "All these years we've 'bound' you," he said. "We've done all we could to separate you. Now God has told us to 'loose' you. We are going to bless you. If you want to get married, we are going to bless that, too."

They looked at each other in amazement. Slowly Jerry's ever-present scowl turned into a grin. "You really mean it?"

"We really mean it," I said. "Jamie's parents did everything they could to keep us apart because they didn't approve of me. But when they loosed us, when they started blessing our relationship rather than cursing it, everything changed."

It was a tough decision, for in the flesh we didn't see any hope for the marriage to work out. But over the next eight months before the wedding, we watched Jerry become who Sandy had said he was all along—a man of God. His violence, which we now realize was his only defense against our disapproval, disappeared. In its place emerged a kind, polite Christian gentleman who has made a wonderful husband for our daughter—just as she had faith to believe.[1]

Sandy finished college after their marriage and now teaches kindergarten in a Christian school. Jerry is a firefighter. They have two precious sons whom their grandmother, Jackie, just adores. The turning point came when Jamie finally said to Jackie, "Let's loose them." From then on they set Sandy and Jerry free—free of judgments, free of expectations, free to be responsible for their own choices. Forgiving and loosing are powerful, liberating "tools" in the hands of loving parents.

Sometimes we feel we've done everything we know to do to rear godly children, then we watch helplessly as they flounder into what seems to be "never-never land." Perhaps we need to explore the possibility: Were they bound by our words and attitudes or someone else's? Releasing them through forgiveness can create the climate for reconciliation.

Our Words Can Bless or Curse

Let's first consider the power of our words. Jamie recognized it was important to release Sandy with a blessing when he realized that binding and loosing is linked to an Old Testament concept of cursing and blessing. He believed his and Jackie's negative words and attitudes, in a sense, had cursed or bound Sandy and Jerry. What they needed was to be loosed and blessed!

Jamie recalled the account in Deuteronomy when God told Moses to curse the enemy and bless God's people. Moses prepared the Israelites to enter the Promised Land by giving them God's orders:

> See, I am setting before you today a blessing and a curse—the blessing if you obey the commands of the Lord your God...the curse if you disobey the commands of the Lord your God...by following other gods, which you have not known (Deuteronomy 11:26-28).

Moses gave instructions that certain tribes were to stand on Mount Gerizim to pronounce the blessings and other designated tribes were to stand on Mount Ebal to pronounce the curses. The people agreed with God, saying, "Amen," or "So be it."

They recognized that obedience would bring blessing; disobedience would cause the curses to come upon them (see Deuteronomy 27:14-26). Their words were binding because God says His Word stands.

Our spoken words can be like blessings or curses—to heal or to hurt. The Bible tells us, "The tongue has the power of life and death" (Proverbs 18:21). Most parents have little understanding of the spiritual power inherent in the words we speak to our children, either for good or for ill. In our years of parenting, most of us probably have unintentionally cursed our children with the negative words we have spoken.

It's easy to do. In a heated moment, without thinking, we can say such things as, "You dummy! You don't have any more sense than your granddaddy." Or, "Bobby, you're lazy just like your shiftless Uncle Bob. You'll never amount to anything either." Or, "You'll never do well in math. I never did, and you're just like me."

A Family Blessing

In their book, *The Blessing,* authors Gary Smalley and John Trent say a family blessing includes:

- Meaningful touch
- A spoken message
- Attaching "high value" to the one being blessed
- Picturing a special future for the one being blessed
- An active commitment to fulfill the blessing[2]

According to Smalley and Trent, the verb "to bless" in Hebrew means to bow the knee, to show reverence or to esteem the person as valuable.[3] The dictionary defines "bless" or "blessing" as wishing a person favor, wholeness, benefit, happiness, prosperity. The words occur in the Bible several hundred times.

The word "curse" appears in various forms in the Bible more than 150 times. The Hebrew word translated "curse" means to make light, of little weight, to bring into contempt, to despise or to dishonor.[4]

A minister friend of mine explains that blessings and curses are usually instigated by words. These words, when spoken, written or formed inwardly and believed by the one speaking, can sometimes produce lasting effects, either for good or for evil.

When we make a negative statement about our children, it's possible that we set in operation a "word curse." As the following illustration shows, others may unwittingly curse our children in the same way.

He Is Not a Bad Boy

As Joan walked into the church day-care center one afternoon to pick up her two-year-old son, she overheard the nursery worker say, "Bart, you are a bad, bad boy."

Joan wasted no time telling her, "I want you to make that right with Bart. Correct his behavior, but don't let your words wound his spirit. He was wrong to take the other child's toy, and he should be told. But please, don't ever tell him he is a bad boy. He's a child of the King, and he made a mistake, but he's not a bad boy."

Bart is truly blessed! His mother understands that discipline is essential for his behavioral development, but she doesn't want him wounded by being told he is "bad." She wants him to grow up blessed!

Words Can Be Binding

Sometimes we parents watch, almost horrified, as our children become what they've heard spoken about them much of their lives. We see behavior traits we abhor and wonder why and how this could be.

Mona's mother, on more than one occasion, had shouted at her, "You are incorrigible, Mona. Someday you'll have a daughter who will sass you back like you do me!"

"Mom, I hate you!" 16-year-old Mona would scream back. "You don't understand me—you don't even try. I'm going to be an understanding mom when I have kids. You wait and see!"

Mona pushed the memory of these shouting matches into the back of her mind until one afternoon at a Texas conference where she sat in on my teaching workshop. She heard me tell of the necessity of breaking words spoken over us or our children. In the hotel lobby afterwards, she asked if I'd pray with her.

"My youngest daughter reacted to me like I did to my mom, and I have resented her for it," she said. "I need to get things right with her. Before Mom died, I became a Christian and went to her hospital room to ask forgiveness for my rebellious teenage years. She released me with forgiveness. I desperately need to do that for my daughter."

Revoking the Words

We prayed together and Mona forgave her daughter. She asked God for an opportunity to explain the need to "break off" her grandmother's words that had bound her. Five months later, a jubilant Mona called me from Texas.

"God answered our prayer," she reported. "My visit with my daughter was wonderful. She was open to my praying with her.

Just as Jesus took the children, put His hands on them and blessed them, we can hold our children—touching, blessing and praying over them.

After talking for hours, we've come to a new understanding of each other. We revoked the words my mom had spoken over me—that I would have an incorrigible daughter—and we've forgiven one another."

"Did you see results?" I asked.

"Yes, an amazing thing has happened since then," she answered. "All three of my children and my husband have recommitted their lives to the Lord. It's absolutely wonderful how God is moving in our family."

When we see the power of words that curse—that make light of or dishonor someone made in the image of God—we begin to understand how our negative words affect our children. It stirs us to change. We want to impart blessings to them with our words.

Just as Jesus took the children, put his hands on them and blessed them—when the disciples wanted to send them away—we can hold our children in our arms, touching, blessing and praying over them.

Blessing the Children

From Old Testament times to now, the tradition of the father blessing the children has been an important part of Jewish family life. It was a duty of parents toward their children and has continued as a regular part of the rabbis' duties toward children on Shabat (the Sabbath) and on feast and holy days.[5]

In blessing their children, the patriarchs attached a high value to their offspring, who in turn greatly desired their blessing. Abraham spoke a blessing to his son Isaac. Isaac blessed Jacob. Jacob blessed his 12 sons and two grandsons.[6] The spoken blessing was accompanied by laying hands on the children. When Joseph brought his two sons to his elderly father, the patriarch kissed and embraced them and stretched out his hand and blessed them with words that spoke of their future.

Before Moses' death, he again pronounced a blessing over each individual tribe of Israel—the families, clans, all the people of God (see Deuteronomy 33).

Remember how disappointed Esau was when he let his brother Jacob rob him of the firstborn blessing? "Bless me—me too, my father!" he begged his father. "Haven't you reserved any blessing for me?" (see Genesis 27:34,36). Esau received a blessing, but not the cherished one Isaac gave Jacob.

When children in biblical times received their father's blessing, it gave them a sense of being highly valued by their parents. They felt assured of a successful future. Today in orthodox Jewish homes, the children still receive their father's blessings on a regular basis.[7]

Children Are Gifts from God

Why all this emphasis on blessing our children? We need to be clear on the point that children are entrusted to us from God as gifts. "Behold, children are a gift of the Lord; The fruit of the womb is a reward" (Psalm 127:3, *NASB*).

One way we show our children they are accepted as gifts from God is to affirm them with our blessings, which includes speaking lovingly to them. Often this can be accompanied by a hug, kiss or touch.

To bless our children also involves recognizing each one's individual talents and helping each child develop in those areas. It's what Smalley and Trent call "an active commitment to fulfill the blessing."

When two of our children were quite young, we discovered they liked art, so we gave them private art lessons. In college, one studied interior design; the other, graphic arts. Both required art training. Our youngest got lots of books because she liked to read. She later worked in a library.

We had no clue this was part of a blessing. As parents, we were just helping them explore and develop their God-given interests, talents and creative bents.

A pastor friend and his wife found a way to honor and bless their five children. Each month they featured a different child by displaying on the kitchen wall things of special significance to the one being singled out for recognition.

A large, recent photo of the child was usually surrounded by smaller pictures of that child when younger. In addition, the child's favorite Scripture, along with any artwork or exceptional recognition received in school was also exhibited. It was like "This Is Your Life" for a whole month. I loved to drop by and see how creative the parents were in rearranging the wall photos whenever it was time for another child to be honored.

Every child needs to know that God is personally concerned with his or her life and welfare and that he or she is of infinite value to Him. Each child needs to feel that his parents regard him in this same way.

Today you hear more and more parents imparting blessings to their children during their wedding ceremonies. My husband spoke blessings over all three of our children at their weddings. I had the privilege of praying and speaking Bible promises over one of our daughters and a niece at theirs.

Can we, like the Buckinghams who shared their story at the beginning of this chapter, forgive, loose and bless our children? Can we free them of our judgments and unreasonable expectations? Can we bless them with our words? With our touch? With our affirmations of their God-given talents?

Yes! With God's help and His creative ideas we can! Most of all, we can keep on praying for God to work in their lives, accomplishing His will and purpose.

Prayer for Ideas

Lord, thank You for my children. Please inspire me with ways to show them my love and Yours. I want them to feel appreciated. I want to help and encourage them to develop and use the gifts You have endowed them with in the best way possible—without being manipulative or controlling. I want to bless them in ways that will be meaningful to each individually. Help me! In Jesus' name, amen.

Prayer of Confession and Repentance

Lord Jesus Christ, I acknowledge You as the Son of God, and I thank You for dying on the Cross for my sins. You redeemed me from the curse of sin that I might receive Your blessings. I love You, Lord. I praise You, Lord. I worship You, my Savior. Amen.

Blessing Prayer

Father, I speak the blessings of obedience over my family: We will be blessed in the city and blessed in the country. Our children and all progeny will be blessed, and our means of livelihood will be blessed. Our sustenance and all necessary provisions will be blessed. We will be blessed when we come in and blessed when we go out (see Deuteronomy 28:2-6).

* * * * *

I also speak Aaron's priestly blessing over my family: "The Lord bless you and keep you; the Lord make his face shine upon you and be gracious to you; the Lord turn his face toward you and give you peace" (Numbers 6:24-26). Amen.

* * * * *

The Lord watches over you—
the Lord is your shade at your right hand;
the sun will not harm you by day,
nor the moon by night.
The Lord will keep you from all harm—
he will watch over your life;
The Lord will watch over
your coming and going
both now and forevermore.
(Psalm 121:5-8)

Notes

1. Jackie Buckingham, "Healing the Wounded Heart," *Help, I'm a Pastor's Wife* (Altamonte Springs, Fla.: Creation House, 1987), pp. 259-262. Edited by Michelle Buckingham. Used by permission of the author.
2. Gary Smalley and John Trent, Ph.D., *The Blessing* (Nashville: Thomas Nelson, 1986), p. 24. Used with permission.
3. Ibid., p. 26.
4. James H. Strong, *The New Strong's Exhaustive Concordance of the Bible* (Nashville: Thomas Nelson Publishers, 1984), #7043 Hebrew Reference, p. 103.
5. Gary Smalley and John Trent, *The Blessing*, p. 30.
6. Ibid., p. 26.
7. Ibid., pp. 30, 33.

Chapter Fourteen

Praying for Your Grandchildren

*I have been reminded of your sincere faith, which first
lived in your grandmother Lois and in your mother
Eunice and, I am persuaded, now lives in you also.*

2 TIMOTHY 1:5
(Paul writing to Timothy)

In our mobile society, with probably half of all marriages ending in divorce, grandparents have a deepening responsibility for their grandchildren. Many help raise their grandchildren while the parents work. In some cases, they bear the full responsibility for their children's offspring.

Because of these possibilities, grandparents often directly influence the lives of their grandchildren—positively or negatively. What kind of influence will you be?

In 1820, a tiny baby girl, Frances Jane, became blind when given the wrong eye medication. Instead of becoming bitter as she grew older, she responded to the training of her faithful grandmother, who helped her memorize much of the Bible. From the time she was young until she died in her nineties, there flowed from that granddaughter thousands of hymns and gospel songs.

We know the blind songwriter as Fanny Crosby and often sing some of the songs she left as a legacy: "Blessed Assurance," "All the Way My Savior Leads Me," "Rescue the Perishing" and hundreds of others.

No, never underestimate the virtuous influence of a godly grandmother.

One Grandmother's Influence

My own mom was not only my prime prayer warrior, but she was also a great intercessor for her grandchildren. Ten years before she died, she had a spiritual renewal—a powerful experience with God.

She had been a good mother, single-handedly raising four children. I was 12 years old and the eldest when she was left alone. Mom earned our living running a boarding house in the shadow of the state capitol. Some 40 boarders shared the house. Another 300 or more ate each day in her large dining room. College kids, construction workers and state legislators came for family-style meals, all they could eat for under a dollar.

Although Mother had always attended church on Sundays— and took us with her—she developed a great love for Jesus and a greater desire to pray after her spiritual renewal when she was 62. By then she had 10 grandchildren, spanning in age from crib to junior high.

Whenever you'd ask her, "What's your greatest joy?" she'd wave both hands toward heaven and say, "To praise the Lord and to pray for my 10 grandchildren represented by these 10 fingers."

When they were lonely, depressed or in need of prayer, my children often called her from college with requests such as, "Mother Jewett, I've got such a hard test Friday, and I'm uptight about it. I need you to pray."

Mom would bombard heaven on behalf of that grandchild. She seemed to have spiritual insights about our children that we didn't always have. She felt free to tell us when she thought we should put actions to our prayers.

Once after talking to our son, who admitted he was having difficulty making his bankbook balance, Mom told my husband, "You need to get to that Florida State campus and see your two kids—if for nothing more than to encourage them with your presence. Praise God for their good qualities and stop looking at their faults."

LeRoy couldn't get off work to go, so at 5 A.M. the next day, I headed for Tallahassee with his blessing—and some money for our college senior from his grandmother to make his bank account solvent.

I have no idea how many hours Mom prayed for my children—only God knows. She was both grandmother and granddaddy to them.

While caring for Mom as she was dying of cancer, I would read Scriptures to her during the long nights when she couldn't sleep. She'd give me her input. Once when reading Proverbs 13:22, "A good man leaves an inheritance for his children's children," she told me, "I want to leave them a spiritual inheritance."

"You've done that," I assured her.

When I read, "Children's children are a crown to the aged," from Proverbs 17:6, she managed to say, "My grandchildren are truly my crown right now."

Two of my children, who lived closest, made frequent trips from college to see Mother the last weeks of her life. They sat by her bed as she endured the final stages of the disease, often screaming in pain. It was their turn to pray for her.

"Why does she suffer so?" Keith agonized, weeping on Easter afternoon two days before her death.

"I don't know," I said. "But the Bible says, 'If we endure, we will also reign with him' (2 Timothy 2:12). God still has a purpose for her on earth. I can tell you she still prays for others. I know her well."

Just before Keith graduated, she died. After commencement ceremonies as we stood outside, he clutched his diploma and looked up toward heaven. "I miss Mother Jewett so much. I wish she could have been here today. She helped me earn this with her prayers."

"She knew you'd succeed. She believed in you," I comforted him, wiping tears from my eyes.

A Privilege to Pray

I often compared my mother to young Timothy's grandmother, Lois. The apostle Paul tells us that, from childhood, Timothy had "known the holy Scriptures," which made him "wise for salvation through faith in Christ Jesus" (2 Timothy 3:15). Obviously he learned these from his grandmother, Lois, and his mother, Eunice, because Paul earlier mentions their faith (2 Timothy 1:5).

One grandmother I know prays Scripture prayers aloud for her grandchildren daily. She told me she likes to paraphrase the Psalms, like this: "Lord, guard my grandson, Tom, in all his ways. Be his stronghold in time of trouble. Help him and deliver him from the wicked. Save him because he takes refuge in You" (37:39,40).

My friend Laura prays the same thing for her eight grandchildren—five of whom are "stepgrandchildren." She prays, "Lord, if You have something to say to them through me, show me. Then provide the right opportunity. Otherwise, I leave them in Your hands for You to minister to them in Your most effective way."

Anoint, Bless and Pray for Grandchildren

LeRoy and I have five small grandchildren—ages one year to four years old—now living near us. We delight to pray over them when their parents bring them by.

As soon as two-and-a-half-year-old Lyden Benjamin walks into our house, he heads for the bookcase where the bottle of anointing oil is kept. He takes it to his Papa LeRoy to anoint him with the sign of the Cross. He stands still as his granddad prays over him, asking God's protection, provision, blessing and destiny on him.

Then Lyden Benjamin sticks his tiny finger into the bottle and anoints his Mama Quin, his mother Quinett and his baby sister, Victoria Jewett. "Bless them," he'll say. His cousin, one-year-old Samuel, waits impatiently for his turn for Papa LeRoy to anoint and bless him, too.

Some may view this as a meaningless ritual. For our family, it is a sacred tradition. Not only is the grandfather bestowing a blessing, but he is teaching a young grandson the solemnity of asking God for blessings.

As I watch LeRoy pray over our grandchildren, I'm reminded of Jacob calling Joseph's two sons to him and blessing them before he died. Grandparents in biblical days had much influence on their grandchildren's lives. I'm sure the righteous ones constantly prayed for their grandchildren.

When two of our newborn grandbabies were just home from the hospital, I sang God's Word over them. Now when I stroll them around our neighborhood, I still sing or hum hymns, encouraging them to join in.

Like other grandparents we know, we keep a collection of Christian children's books, videos and cassette tapes at our house. Of course, we read, read, read to ours! Our grandkids love to play their rhythm band instruments, wear biblical costumes and role-play some of the Bible stories they've watched on the videos. Joshua and the walls of Jericho, David and Goliath, Queen Esther and Noah and the ark are among their favorites.

Dedicate Babies to God

Three of our five grandchildren were dedicated to God, either in our home or their parents' home. Grandparents, aunts and uncles were present, when possible, to witness the occasion. My husband read from the Scriptures, and the children's parents promised to give their children a Christian upbringing.

We dressed in our Sunday best to commemorate this extra special celebration. Once the service was over, a big party followed, with cake, refreshments, photos and gifts for the baby as a reminder of his or her dedication day. (For a sample dedication service, see appendix 2.)

This tradition originated when my husband and I invited my grandfather, an elderly retired Presbyterian minister, to our home to pray over our children when they were very young. At the time, I didn't realize the significance of asking him to bless them. But because my grandfather had performed our wedding ceremony, I wanted him to lay hands on our children and pass a blessing on to them. Something in me longed for that, yet I was too immature in my faith to comprehend it all. Now I'm glad I kept insisting that he come to our home in Florida to pronounce three blessings. The photos of those occasions are priceless to me.

Just a few years ago, I attended a memorial service for a beloved pastor—one I will never forget. During the service, his widow, their five children, their spouses and all their grandchildren gathered on the church's platform. The moment had come to dedicate the newest baby, the thirteenth grandchild, to the Lord.

The words of the officiating pastor still ring in my ears: "Moses is dead, but Joshua will inherit the promised land." Joshua was the name of the grandson being dedicated to God—at his grandfather's funeral. Tears spilled down my face at the awesomeness of this occasion.

At another memorial service, the deceased man's "last will and testament" was read. It recounted the Christian heritage passed to him from his parents; then described his own walk with the Lord during his 60 years of life. He challenged his children and grandchildren to continue passing on this spiritual heritage from generation to generation. I listened enthralled. I could just imagine how his children and grandchildren felt even as they were saying their good-byes to the family patriarch. He was already in heaven with his Lord, they were assured. They had a choice to follow, too.

I left both services with new ideas. And a lot of questions.

What legacy was I leaving my children? What could I pass down to my future grandchildren?

*I will often speak over my grandchildren,
"God has a purpose for your life—
a destiny for you to fulfill. I pray for God
to prepare you for that destiny."*

Though my grandchildren are too young to understand the meaning of the words I speak over them, I often say to the one I'm rocking at the moment, "God has a purpose for your life—a destiny for you to fulfill. I pray for God to prepare you for that destiny."

If we have grandchildren, we have the rare privilege of nurturing them in the love of the Lord. But suppose you don't live close by. I can identify. Three of ours were born overseas, so we weren't in their lives from the beginning.

Today in our nation, people are often separated from their families by hundreds of miles. Divorce, in-law problems, financial lack or general alienation often keep grandparents from seeing their grandchildren.

One grandmother, experiencing the heartache of having two of her beloved grandchildren ripped away from her by divorce as the mother took the children across country to relocate, wrote:

> The pain of their leaving lived in the nooks and crannies of my heart until I decided to allow the Holy Spirit to take it away and replace it with hope. In the following weeks, God in his mercy showed me, day by day, that He was in control of the circumstances and that He would take care of me and those I love so dearly. I began to heal and learn that goodbye doesn't necessarily mean forever.[1]

Josephene, who hasn't seen four of her grandchildren in 11 years, shared her heartache. "Two of my daughters got mad at me when I remarried after the death of their Dad. One invented false accusations. So they withdrew. Not only do they not speak to me, they don't allow their children to have any communication, either. Even my letters to my grandchildren are returned.

"I grieved for a long time over this," Josephene says. "But the Lord told me I can't quit living. I'd love to see my grandchildren. I pray for them to come to know the Lord; for the truth of these accusations to be revealed; and for our family to be restored. I pray, but I keep on keeping on with life."

One of my prayer partners spends literally hours each day praying for her grandchildren. Yet several years may pass before she gets to see them.

Those of us who do live near our grandchildren can touch them, bless them and encourage them. We can all have a positive influence in their lives by faithfully praying for them.

"Some of our happiest grandparenting times come when we are truly on fire for the Lord and the children see it, feel it and want to emulate it," according to my friend Irene.[2] I agree. Let's ask God how to pray more effectively for those treasures in our lives.

Prayers for Grandchildren

Lord, I pray all my grandchildren will come to a saving knowledge of Jesus at an early age and stay within the boundaries of Your love and safety.

* * * * *

Lord, show my grandchild that You are able to do immeasurably more than _____(name) can ask or imagine according to Your power that is at work within him/her (see Ephesians 3:20).

* * * * *

May my grandchild ———————— come to know this Scripture personally: "No eye has seen, no ear has heard; no mind has conceived what God has prepared for those who love him" (1 Corinthians 2: 9,10). God, reveal it by Your Spirit to him/her. Amen.

* * * * *

Lord, I pray that my grandchildren, like David, will serve the purpose of God in their generation before they go to be with You (see Acts 13:36).

* * * * *

Teach my grandchild to cast all his cares upon You, God, for You care for him (see 1 Peter 5:7).

* * * * *

I pray that my grandchild ———————— may prosper in all things and be in health, just as his/her soul prospers (see 3 John 2).

* * * * *

Lord, help my grandchild ———————— to develop godly character by speaking truthfully and not telling falsehoods, not stealing, not letting unwholesome talk come out of his/her mouth, and not grieving the Holy Spirit. Help my grandchild to be an imitator of God and live a life of love (see Ephesians 4:25-29; 5:1).

* * * * *

Help my grandchildren to obey their parents in the Lord and to honor them (see Ephesians 6:1).

* * * * *

I pray that You, O Lord, will give Your angels charge over my grandchildren, to guard them in all their ways (see Psalm 91:11).

* * * * *

Lord, I pray my grandchildren will flee from sexual immorality, impurity, greed and disobedience, and not be deceived. Help them to live as children of light, pleasing the Lord (see Ephesians 5:3,5,8).

Notes

1. Irene M. Endicott, *Grandparenting Redefined* (Lynnwood, Wash.: Aglow International, 1992), p. 73.
2. Ibid., p. 190.

Chapter Fifteen

Giving Your Children a Prayer Heritage

Only be careful, and watch yourselves closely so that you do not forget the things your eyes have seen or let them slip from your heart as long as you live. Teach them to your children and to their children after them.

DEUTERONOMY 4:9

If we want our children to pray, they must hear us pray. There is no greater demonstration of God's power to our children than when they see their own parents receive answers to prayer. This happens when they hear us pray and witness the results.

An Answer for Kent

"I can't sleep. I can't sleep," my nephew Kent sobbed as he stood by my bed at 3 A.M. "Come stay with me again," he begged.

I scooped him up and trudged off toward the boys' room for the third time that night. My sister had left her five-year-old with us while their family was overseas for three weeks. But none of us slept much. Inevitably he'd wake up screaming from a bad dream. I'd rock him or sit beside his bed until he'd fall asleep again. After several nights of this, I was exhausted.

One afternoon when my mother's minister, Forrest Mobley, stopped by for a chat, I mentioned Kent's sleeplessness. "We've tried everything. He just won't sleep through the night. We don't know what to do," I told him.

"I think I know what you are going through," he said. A spark of hope rose within me as he continued. "A few weeks ago, parents in our congregation had the same problem with their son. God gave us an answer."

"He did?"

"The Lord showed me a Scripture to share with them. I told the parents to have their son repeat the verse at the end of his prayers each night. And he stopped having nightmares."

"What was it?" I asked, moving to the edge of the couch so I wouldn't miss a word.

"Simply this: 'Father, into Your hands I commit my spirit.'"

"Why, that's what Jesus said when He hung on the Cross," I replied.

"Yes, He was committing His spirit to His heavenly Father. That's what we need to do—to totally commit, or give up, our spirits to God to protect and watch over us while we sleep," he told me.

As he rose to leave, he said, "Remember, God doesn't give us a spirit of fear, but of power, love and a sound mind."

That night I explained some basics to Kent. "Do you believe God takes care of you at night while you sleep?" I asked him.

"Well, my mommy told me He does," he answered.

"Kent, God never sleeps. He says so in the Bible. If He is watching over you while you sleep, you don't have anything to be afraid of."

"I guess not," he said.

"Tonight I want to teach you a new Bible verse. You can repeat it each night with your prayers. Say, 'Father, into Your hands I commit my spirit.'"

Kent repeated it, haltingly at first, then with more confidence.

"That's fine, Kent. Now I want you to remember, God is going to watch over you and protect you. He's going to give you sound sleep tonight. Close your eyes and thank Him for doing it."

He obeyed and, to my astonishment, within minutes Kent was sleeping soundly. The next night when I sat on the edge of his bed as he prayed, he said his new verse again. He went to sleep without begging for me to stay at his bedside, and slept peacefully all night. In fact, he slept through every night after that while we kept him.

That summer I learned a lot about God's plan for His children's restful sleep. I have since shared this incident and some Scriptures with many parents desiring to pray with their children regarding nightmares.[1]

Hannah's Legacy

The Bible gives us many examples of prayer. Let's study Hannah's prayer for a moment—the one she breathed in silence in the temple as the priest Eli watched. Her lips moved, but her voice was not heard. Eli thought she was drunk. Yet what she said to God was recorded, no doubt because she later told Samuel what she had prayed.

Hannah wept much and prayed to the Lord, saying, "O Lord Almighty, if you will only look upon your servant's misery and...give her a son, then I will give him to the Lord for all the days of his life" (1 Samuel 1:10,11).

Hers is the first recorded prayer of a woman in the Old Testament. Her request was specific: "Give me a son." She asked God to change her barrenness. Three times she humbled herself, calling herself a "servant." Unselfish in her petition, she vowed to give her child back to God.

Hannah was honest in her prayer. She meant business with God. She even risked being misunderstood by the priest who told her to get rid of her wine.

Hannah replied, "I am a woman who is deeply troubled. I have not been drinking...I was pouring out my soul to the Lord" (1 Samuel 1:15).

The priest answered, "Go in peace, and may the God of Israel grant you what you have asked of him" (v. 17).

In the course of time, Hannah conceived and gave birth to a son whom she named Samuel, saying, "Because I asked the Lord for him" (v. 20).

By the time of her next recorded prayer, Hannah has matured in her prayer life. She begins with her feelings but ends by prais-

*What a heritage Hannah left
her son, Samuel! And we have the
opportunity to leave our children
that same legacy of prayer.*

ing God for His power, His righteousness. Finally, she prophesies that God will give strength to His king—in a land which had never had a king before. Eventually, her firstborn son, Samuel, would anoint Israel's first king (see 1 Samuel 2:1-11).

Sometimes we forget that Hannah had three sons and two daughters born after Samuel. Truly God did answer her prayers!

Samuel's name came from two Hebrew words—one, the word for God; the other meaning, "I ask." Every time she called his name, Hannah was saying, "I asked God." Surely he knew from earliest childhood his mother's prayers were answered. (One of our grandsons is named Samuel for this very reason.)

What a heritage Hannah left her son. And we have the opportunity to leave our children that same legacy.

In meditating on Mary's prayer before the birth of Jesus, we can see that it resembles Hannah's magnificent praise prayer. Because these women's prayers are recorded, they can serve as patterns for us to pray aloud. This also encourages us to write down our prayers to leave for our children and their children after them.

Traditions and Prayer Go Together

One of the ways we can pray and teach our children—even if they are grown—is to establish some family traditions. It's never too late, especially in your own home.

Traditions help preserve memories. In Psalms, we are admonished to tell of God's mighty deeds from generation to generation. Note this Scripture:

> I will utter hidden things, things from of old—what we have heard and known, what our fathers have told us. We will not hide them from their children; we will tell the next generation the praiseworthy deeds of the Lord, his power, and the wonders he has done...so the next generation would know them, even the children yet to be born, and they in turn would tell their children (Psalm 78:2,3,4,6).

Traditions exist in every household, whether we recognize them as that or not. These are things we do habitually every year, things we teach our children and pass on to them. Sharing oral stories of our childhood, our parents' childhood and even our grandparents' can be fun, entertaining and special. Most importantly however, is our need to share our Christian values, our roots and heritage. We are to teach them to our children and our grandchildren.

As far back as Old Testament times the Israelites were fervent tradition-keepers, enjoying their celebrations, feasts and festivals—holy days.

Celebrating Our Jewish Roots

After our daughter Quinett had lived in Israel, she came home with the suggestion that our family start celebrating some aspects of Passover week, but with a Messianic emphasis.

We all know the story of the wicked Egyptian Pharaoh who

would not free the Jews from slavery, even when God's messenger, Moses, told him to let the people go. God sent 10 plagues to break Pharaoh's resistance, but Pharaoh's heart was hardened. Finally, when the angel of death killed the firstborn son in every Egyptian home, the tyrant released the Israelites. The death angel "passed over" Jewish homes where the blood of an unblemished lamb had been smeared on the doorframes (see Exodus 12:1-13). Thus the Passover became one of the most important religious holidays on the Jewish calendar.

We who have trusted Jesus as our Messiah believe He is the blameless Lamb of God. His death, burial and resurrection opened the way for God to forgive our sins and to abolish the system requiring continual sacrificial offerings.

Nine years ago we began the tradition of sharing a *Seder*, the ceremonial Passover meal, in recognition of the Jewish roots of our Christian faith, while also celebrating Christ's death and resurrection. We do this in the spring around Easter, but not always on the day of the Jewish Passover.

With fresh candles in our menorah, all our family—including our little ones dressed in Israeli costumes—and a few invited guests celebrate this almost two-hour ceremony. Quinett and I prepare all the food according to Jewish recipes and tradition. Different persons at our table participate in reading the Scriptures and prayers.

We use *The Messianic Passover Haggadah* booklet written in Hebrew and English.[2] *Haggadah* means "the telling," and the messianic version of this teaching tool explains the rich meaning of this wonderful, joyous celebration.

New Year's Eve

For 17 years now, we've spent New Year's Eve reviewing the year that's about to end. It's a favorite family tradition.

We go around the room, giving each one an opportunity to share how God has intervened or answered prayer during the year. We praise and pray, giving God the glory for the diverse victories in our lives. Finishing with our "praise reports," we then have holy communion, followed by a time of celebration.

Somewhere down the street, fireworks explode. A new year has begun. Time to start a new prayer diary. Time to trust God for more miraculous answers to prayers.

An Affirmation of Love

For years I've made it a tradition to write my three children a letter at Christmastime. It's both a love letter and a "bless you" letter. I encourage each to use the special gifts God has given him or her to His glory. I share Scriptures I will be praying for them in the year ahead. I know it's important to bless our children often with words, both spoken and written, and this is one way I can do it.

Each of us need to pass on to the next generation things that are important and invaluable. The last Christmas my mother was alive, she told us stories of her childhood as we recorded them on tape. Even now we can laugh along with her when I play the cassette to introduce my own grandchildren to her wit.

Because she knew it was probably her last Christmas with us, she had me wrap a few of her personal things to give to her grandchildren on Christmas morning. She wanted to see their expressions as they opened their boxes to see what she had chosen for each—her Bibles, small pieces of jewelry, special coins, several oil paintings she had done of her beloved Destin, Florida.

Four months before she died, she wrote a letter to her four children—her farewell. "I've felt the joy of the Lord and His grace and know that peace which passes all understanding will sustain and carry me through," she wrote. "So to each of you, I trust this will be an opportunity and not an ordeal. I desire you to know God's grace is sufficient for you." How I treasure her last written words to me. I'll pass them along to her great-granddaughter named for her.

Write Family History

Two years ago, I wrote our family's life story for my children so they can later pass it on to their children. They will know of their spiritual heritage from their parents and ancestors, as well as their Scottish background from my side and their German roots from their father.

It's never too late to start a "Christian tradition." I believe it goes hand in hand with praying for our children, because it is passing on to them something very distinctive from your own family.

A Scripture that inspired me to do this is Deuteronomy 4:9: "Only be careful, and watch yourselves closely so that you do not forget the things your eyes have seen or let them slip from your heart as long as you live. Teach them to your children and to their children after them."

Let Them Hear You Pray

Charles Spurgeon wrote that his own conversion was a result of prayer—the long, affectionate, earnest and importunate prayer of his parents. He heard their prayers. God also heard their cries. And Spurgeon became one of the most noted British preachers of the nineteenth century.

The Scriptures clearly admonish Christian parents to instruct their children in the ways of God. We are told to teach His commandments to our children, to talk about them when we sit at home and when we walk along the road, when we lie down and when we get up (see Deuteronomy 6:7). I believe this includes praying aloud for them so they can hear us, when we lie down at night or arise in the morning.

A Covenant of Love

I get excited every time I read the verse that says God keeps "his covenant of love to a thousand generations of those who love him and keep his commands" (Deuteronomy 7:9). What an inheritance that is!

Let us pass on to our children the greatest heritage possible—our personal prayer lives after which they can model their own. I've watched my adult children almost outdistance me in prayer in recent years. Since becoming parents, they've learned the importance of praying earnestly for those little ones God has entrusted to them. Together we can teach their children to pray.

Through our prayers, our children and grandchildren can become powerhouses to change the world. Among them may be evangelists, preachers, teachers and missionaries who will help to bring salvation to our world. Others will be great musicians whose songs will melt hard, unbelieving hearts. Some will be writers, editors and publishers of Christian materials. Still others will be community or national leaders who will promote godliness in government at all levels.

We need believers in every field of work to reach others for Christ. Some of our children will be engineers, architects, lawyers, health care workers, waitresses, chefs, clerks, artists, store owners, administrators, computer programmers, dramatists, construction workers, bankers, grocers, law enforcement officials—whatever God's call on their lives may be.

Strengthened by the Holy Spirit and supported by the prayers of believing parents, godly young people can accomplish feats they never dreamed possible. God is looking for committed people through whom He can change the world and our sons and daughters could be the ones He will use.

Let's pray they will influence an ungodly world—revealing Christ to their fellow students, teachers or workmates—becoming salt and light to their generation.

We, like Joshua, can declare both by our words and by our actions, "As for me and my household, we will serve the Lord" (Joshua 24:15).

Only God knows what will happen if we Christian parents truly pray for our children and leave footprints of faith for them to follow.

Scriptures for Meditation

May your deeds be shown to your servants, your splendor to their children (Psalm 90:16).

* * * * *

The children of your servants will live in your presence; their descendants will be established before you (Psalm 102:28).

* * * * *

Blessed is the man who fears the Lord, who finds great delight in his commands. His children will be mighty in the land; the generation of the upright will be blessed (Psalm 112:1,2).

* * * * *

He who fears the Lord has a secure fortress, and for his children it will be a refuge (Proverbs 14:26).

* * * * *

I am the Lord, I have called you in righteousness, I will also hold you by the hand and watch over you. Behold, the former things have come to pass, now I declare new things; before they spring forth I proclaim them to you (Isaiah 42:6,9, *NASB*).

* * * * *

I will pour out my Spirit on your offspring, and my blessing on your descendants (Isaiah 44:3).

* * * * *

Yes, captives will be taken from warriors, and plunder retrieved from the fierce; I will contend with those who contend with you, and your children I will save (Isaiah 49:25)

* * * * *

In my faithfulness I will reward them [my people] and make an everlasting covenant with them. Their descendants will be known among the nations and their offspring among the peoples. All who see them will acknowledge that they are a people the Lord has blessed (Isaiah 61:8,9).

* * * * *

I am the Lord, the God of all mankind. Is anything too hard for me? (Jeremiah 32:27).

Notes
1. Scriptures on sleep include Proverbs 3:24,25a; Psalm 121:3b; Psalm 127:2.
2. Lederer Publications, 6240 Park Heights Ave., Baltimore, MD 21215. This company publishes other material to help Christian adults and children celebrate the various Jewish feasts.

Epilogue

This decade has seen innumerable Christian parents awakened to the spiritual battle raging over our children. We've always known we should pray for our children, but often we've unfairly judged them and we have not shown them mercy (see James 2:13). Now more and more parents perceive Satan's intent to steal, kill and destroy their children.

Prayer—along with spiritual nurturing—is our greatest defense against this evil assault. For those who have been taken captive, our prayers become offensive warfare invading the camp of the enemy. By using the scriptural weapons God provides, we can take back from the adversary what he has stolen from us. But often the battle is difficult and costly.

During many years of teaching on spiritual warfare, I've prayed with hundreds of distraught parents whose children had rebelled and gone over to the enemy's camp. "Change her heart, Lord!" they plead. "Oh God, turn his steps back toward you!"

Eventually they discover, as both Quin and I have, that we as parents must be willing to change before we can see metamorphosis in our children's lives. When we truly open ourselves to the work of the Holy Spirit, He reveals the deep, hidden motives of our hearts—motives often rooted in pride.

One mother I know shared her anguish over her teenage son's rebellion. He had taken up with ungodly friends, bleached his hair, refused for years to get a haircut, then got his ear pierced. She cried out to God to change her son.

In prayer one day, her heart was stricken when she sensed

the Lord saying to her, "Do you want an inside job or an outside job? Will it help to change his outward appearance if there's no change of heart?"

Realizing that her anger and embarrassment over her son's appearance were part of her motive in asking God to change him, she confessed her sin of unforgiveness and spiritual pride. Her prayer became, "Lord, help me express Your love to my son. Do whatever it takes to turn his heart toward You."

Next, the Holy Spirit convicted her about her judgment and anger toward her son's companions, whom she felt had led him astray. She had no compassion for them, nor any interest in praying for their salvation. As God continued to reveal her sinful attitudes, she asked God to change her own heart.

This mother learned a painful, but vital, lesson: Anger, unforgiveness and spiritual pride hinder our prayers from being answered. And once they *are* answered, we must free our children to follow the Lord's leading in their lives.

If we but ask, God can help us see beyond outward appearances. He will enable us to love unconditionally, pray faithfully and stand against the enemy relentlessly. Our spiritual warfare on behalf of our children will then become effective and powerful, and the Lord can instill in us a deep desire to pray for the children of others.

I pray you, dear reader, will overcome the enemy's scheme to neutralize your effectiveness in praying for your children. Then take your place in the spiritual battle to see total victory in their lives.

—*Ruthanne Garlock*

APPENDICES

Prayers to Pray for Your Children

Following are some Scripture intercessions I pray for my children:

Dedication

Lord, as You did for Hannah, take this child of mine, _____ . I give him/her to You. For his/her whole life, he/she will be given over to You (see 1 Samuel 1:28).

Deliverance

I thank You that "the seed of the righteous shall be delivered" (Proverbs 11:21, *KJV*). Lord, I am righteous because of Jesus' shed blood. My children are my seed, and they shall be delivered. Thank You in advance for this promise.

Father, I thank You that You will deliver _____ from the evil one and guide him in paths of righteousness for Your name's sake (see Matthew 6:13; Psalm 23:3).

Forgiveness

Thank You, Father, that the blood of Jesus purifies us from all sin. Thank You that _____ has asked for your forgiveness and cleansing. Now help _____ forget what is behind and strain toward what is ahead, pressing on toward the goal to win the prize for which God has called him/her heavenward in Christ Jesus (see 1 John 1:7,9; Philippians 3:13,14).

Future

I thank You, Lord, that You know the plans You have for _____ are to prosper and not to harm him/her, but to give him/her hope and a future. I pray that _____ will not walk in the counsel of the wicked, or stand in the way of sinners, or sit in the seat of mockers. Instead, I pray that _____ 's delight will be in the law of the Lord and he/she will meditate on it day and night (see Jeremiah 29:11; Psalm 1).

Future Mate for a Daughter

Lord, may _____ 's future husband love the Lord with all his heart, soul, mind and strength, and know Jesus as his personal Lord and Savior (see Mark 12:30; Romans 10:9).

May he love his wife with a faithful, undying love for as long as they both shall live (see Matthew 19:5,6). May he recognize his body as the temple of the Holy Spirit and treat it wisely (see 1 Corinthians 6:19,20). May he be healthy, able to work and support a family (see 1 Timothy 6:8).

May he have an admirable goal in life (see Matthew 6:33). May he use his talents wisely and release his wife to use her God-given talents, also. May their talents complement one another (see Matthew 25:14-30). May they enjoy doing things together.

May he establish their home in accordance with God's prescribed order as outlined in Ephesians 5:20-28. May he be strong in mind, and may the two of them be compatible intellectually (see 2 Corinthians 13:11). May he be a good money manager.

Lord, bring this partner into my daughter's life in Your perfect timing. May they be in love with each other—and both of them in love with You, O God. Let there be no doubt You created them for each other as long as they both shall live. In Jesus' name, amen.

Future Mate for a Son

Lord, may they be equally yoked in every way (see 2 Corinthians 6:14). May she love the Lord God with all her heart, soul, mind and strength. May she embrace Jesus as her personal Savior and Lord (see Mark 12:30; Romans 10:9).

May she love my son with an undying love as long as they both shall live, and be "a helper suitable for him" (Genesis 2:18). May she be rich in good deeds, generous and hospitable (see 1 Timothy 6:18; Hebrews 13:2).

May she encourage my son daily (see Hebrews 3:13). May she use her God-given talents at home and in Your kingdom's work (see Matthew 25:14-30). If housework ever seems to be a monotonous chore to her, help her realize that whatever she does, in word or deed, she should do it with all her heart as working for You (see Colossians 3:17,23).

When they have a family, help her be a good mother. May her children "arise and call her blessed" (Proverbs 31:28). Show her how to prepare nutritious meals for her family. If she needs to learn something about homemaking, help her not to be shy about asking more mature Christian women to help her (Titus 2:3-5).

(P.S. Help me be a good mother-in-law to this precious one.)

In Jesus' name, amen.

Health

Father, I thank You that Jesus took our infirmities and carried our sorrows. And thank You that by His wounds we are healed. I pray that, in all respects, _____ may enjoy good health and that all may go well with him/her, even as his/her soul is getting along well. I thank You for Your promise to sustain _____ on his/her sickbed and restore him/her from the bed of illness (see Isaiah 53:4,5; 3 John 2; Psalm 41:3).

Learning

May my child, like Daniel, show "aptitude for every kind of learning," be "well informed, quick to understand, and qualified to serve in the king's palace" (Daniel 1:4).

Help my child, like Solomon, to have wisdom and great discernment and breadth of understanding "as measureless as the sand on the seashore" (1 Kings 4:29).

Life's Work

Lord, fill _____ with the knowledge of Your will through all spiritual wisdom and understanding, so that he/she lives a life worthy of You, to please You in every way (see Colossians 1:9,10).

Maturity

Dear Father, may _____ , like Your Son Jesus, grow in wisdom and stature, and in favor with You and with the people his/her life touches. Give _____ a listening ear to parental instructions. Help him/her to pay attention that he/she may gain understanding (see Luke 2:52; Proverbs 4:1).

May my child walk "in a manner worthy of the Lord, to please Him in all respects, bearing fruit in every good work and increasing in the knowledge of God" (Colossians 1:10, *NASB*).

Needs

Thank You, dear Father, that You will supply all of _____ 's needs according to Your glorious riches in Christ Jesus (see Philippians 4:19).

Petition

Lord, with thanksgiving I present my requests to You today on behalf of my children, _____

_____

(name the children and your requests). I speak them with my mouth, believe them with my heart, and thank You in advance for hearing me. I pray in Jesus' name, amen (see Philippians 4:6; Mark 11:23).

Protection

Thank You, dear God, that You will command Your angels concerning _____ to guard him/her in all his/her ways. Protect him/her from stumbling, both physically and spiritually (see Psalm 91:11,12).

Lord, guard my children from wrong influences, wrong friends and wrong environment. Bring the right friends into their lives at the right time.

Salvation

Father, You are not willing that _____ should be lost, but that this child come to repentance. Lord Jesus, I thank You that You came to save the lost, including _____ and me. I thank You in advance that _____ will become a believer in You (see Matthew 18:14; 2 Peter 3:9).

I thank you that all my children, _____

_____, shall be taught of the

Lord and great shall be their peace (see Isaiah 54:13).

Spiritual Growth

Father, give_____ the Spirit of wisdom and revelation, so that he/she may know You better. I pray the
eyes of his/her heart may be enlightened in order that
he/she may know the hope to which You have called
him/her. May _____ understand the riches of the
glorious inheritance he/she has in You, and Your incompa-
rably great power for us who believe. I pray Christ may
dwell in his/her heart through faith and that he/she may be
rooted and established in love (see Ephesians 1:17,19; 3:17).

Temptation

Thank You, dear Father, that You know how to rescue
_____ from temptation and trials. I pray he/she
will flee the evil desires of youth, and pursue righteousness, faith, love and peace, along with those who call on
You out of a pure heart. I pray _____will have
nothing to do with stupid arguments, because we know
they produce quarrels. I ask that_____will keep
his/her way pure by living according to Your Word, hid-
ing it in his/her heart (see 2 Peter 2:9; 2 Timothy 2:22,23;
Psalm 119:9-11).

My Daughter-in-Law's Prayers for Her Children

My son, Keith, and his wife, Dana, pray for their daughters,
Kara, 4, and Evangeline, 2, with great fervor. Some prayers are
"preventive praying." I firmly believe their daughters never
have to venture into the paths of rebellion but can stay firmly
within God's boundaries of protection and love. Some of these
are "waiting prayers" planted for their future.

These are the prayers my daughter-in-law brought me to pray in agreement with her and my son:

1. That they would have the unfading beauty of a gentle and quiet spirit (see 1 Peter 3:4).
2. That they would have cheerfully obedient spirits (see Ephesians 6:1,2).
3. That the Lord would protect them—body, soul, spirit— against danger, harm and evil (see 1 Thessalonians 5:23; Psalm 91:14).
4. That they would be filled with the fruits of the Spirit (see Galatians 5:22-24).
5. That they would know Jesus is their best friend and that they can tell Him everything.
6. That they would fall in love with the Lord and enjoy Him and, in turn, lead many to love Him.
7. That they would know Mommy and Daddy love and accept them no matter what they do.
8. We claim their lives for salvation and redemption.
9. We pray they will have discernment and wisdom to choose the paths of righteousness.
10. We pray they will influence people for good and for God wherever they go.
11. We pray that, in every season of their lives, the Lord will give them godly friends who will influence them for the Lord.
12. We pray Psalm 121, that the Lord would be their keeper.
13. We pray that they will know early in life what their destiny is and that we as parents (and grandparents) will nurture that purpose and their giftings with wisdom.
14. We pray that the Lord would keep them and their future husbands for each other, and that their husbands will be raised in godly homes and choose righteous paths.

Dedication of a Baby

At the dedication services my husband conducted for our seven-day-old granddaughter in the home of her parents, he followed this general outline. However, he stopped to add his comments to the parents from time to time.

Family members gathered around the baby cradled in her mother's arms—and sometimes in her daddy's arms when she squirmed.

Our Service

"The Bible says, 'I will pour out My Spirit on your offspring, and My blessing on your descendants' (Isaiah 44:3, *NASB*). Today we stand on that promise that God will pour out his blessing on this precious new baby.

"Quinett and Michael, you are coming to dedicate Victoria Jewett to the Lord as witnessed by our family gathered around you. I want to ask you some questions.

"Do you acknowledge Jesus as your Lord and Savior?"

Answer: "I do."

"Do you renounce the devil and all his works?"

Answer: "I do."

"Do you promise to raise this child in the nurture and admonition of the Lord?"

Answer: "Yes, I do."

"We come to dedicate Victoria, asking that 'the Spirit of the Lord shall rest upon [her]—the Spirit of wisdom and of understanding, the Spirit of counsel and might, the Spirit of knowledge and of the reverential and obedient fear of the Lord' (Isaiah 11:2, *Amp.*). Let's pray:

Heavenly Father, we ask You to send angels to protect Victoria and for the Holy Spirit to teach and guide her. May Jesus always be her best friend. May she, like Jesus, increase in wisdom and stature and in favor with God and man. Your Kingdom come, Your will be done in her life, Lord.

"Do family members gathered here promise to help this child to grow up in a Christian environment?"

Answer: "We will, with God's help."

"Victoria, I anoint you with oil in the name of the Father, the Son and the Holy Spirit and ask God's richest blessings on you all the days of your life."

Victoria's grandfather took her from her mother, then lifted her up to God and pronounced a final scriptural blessing over her:

> The Lord will keep you from all harm—
> He will watch over your life;
> The Lord will watch over
> your coming and going
> both now and forevermore
> (Psalm 121:7,8).

The Lord bless you and keep you;
The Lord make his face shine
upon you and be gracious to you;
the Lord turn his face toward
youand give you peace
(Numbers 6:24,25).

Then the mother and father each lifted her up in dedication to Him.

Appendix III

Worship Helps

Worship is a good starting place for any prayer time, as mentioned in chapter 1. When we come to worship God we are coming to bow down, to give reverence, to humbly beseech our Creator. We acknowledge who God is and we come in humility and love to adore Him.

Often I go through the alphabet and concentrate on the characteristics of the Trinity—God's goodness as our Father; Jesus, His Son, who died for our sins; and the Holy Spirit, our advocate and teacher. Then I add my thanks aloud, naming things about the Godhead for which I am forever grateful. You can add others to this short list.

A: Almighty God, Abba Father, Alpha and Omega, All-Sufficient One, Awesome God, the I Am, Always Available, Ancient of Days.

B: Bread of Life, Bright and Morning Star, Blood of the Lamb, Beginning and the End, Breath of Life, Beautiful, Balm of Gilead, Blessing and honor and glory and power are due Your name.

C: Christ, Covenant Keeper, Consuming Fire, Coming with the clouds, Conquering King.

D: Divine, Deliverer, Destroyer of Sin.

E: Everlasting God, Eternal Light, Excellent, Exalted, Edify, Encourager.

F: Father, Faithful Friend, Forgiver, Faultless, Fortress, Finisher, Fellowships with us, the First and the Last.

G: God of Glory, Grace, Giver of Life, Glorious One, Guide, Guard, Gladness, Great and marvelous are your deeds.

H: Holy One, High Priest, Honorable, Healer, Helper, Heart of love, Harvester, Hope, Hears our prayers, Hosanna, Holy Spirit.

I: Immanuel, I Am, Indescribable, Immortal, Invisible.

J: Jehovah, Jesus, Just and True, Joyful, Judge.

K: King of all kings, Keeper, Kind, Knowing.

L: Lord of lords, Lamb, Lord God Almighty, Living Word, Light of the World, Lamp, Life, Lawgiver, Lion of Judah, Lovely, Lover of my soul.

M: Master, Maker of heaven and earth, Mediator, Magnificent, Majestic, Most High God.

N: Name above all names, Never failing, Nazarene, New mercies every morning, Noble, Narrow Gate, Need-meeter.

O: Omnipotent, Omnipresent, Only Begotten, One God, Omega, Obedient to death.

P: Propitiation, Powerful, Provider, Protector, Patient, Praiseworthy.

Q: Quieter of storms, Quality, Quite a Provider!

R: Righteous, Redeemer, Reigning Monarch, Repairer of the Breach, Restorer, Rock of Salvation, Radiant, Ruler, Ransom from the dead.

S: Savior, Shepherd, Son of God, Son of Man, Supreme, Straight and narrow.

T: True, Truth, Teacher, Transformer, Trustworthy, Triumphal.

U: Unchangeable, Understanding, Unfailing, Universal, Upright.

V: Vine, Victorious, Valuable, Virtuous, Voice of God.

W: Warrior, Worthy, Wise, Who is and Who was and Who is to come, Water, Wind, the Word.

X: Extra-ordinary in all Your ways.

Y: YHWH (Hebrew name for God, Jehovah), Yoke, the Same Yesterday, Today and Tomorrow.

Z: Zealous, Zeal.

Appendix IV

Recommended Books

Haggard, Ted, and Jack Hayford. *Loving Your City into the Kingdom: City-Reaching Strategies for a 21st Century Revival*. Ventura, Calif.: Regal Books, 1997.

Hansen, Jane, with Marie Powers. *Fashioned for Intimacy: Reconciling Men and Women to God's Original Design*. Ventura, Calif.: Regal Books, 1997.

Jacobs, Cindy. *The Voice of God: How God Speaks Personally and Corporately to His Children Today*. Ventura, Calif.: Regal Books, 1995.

———. *Women of Destiny: Discovering God's Great Plan for Your Life*. Ventura, Calif.: Regal Books, 1998.

Lord, Peter. *The 2959 Plan—A Guide to Communion with God*. Titusville, Fla.: Agape Ministries, 1978. This loose-leaf book helps you keep a prayer diary. *2959* is to encourage you to spend "almost" 30 minutes a day with the Lord—29 minutes and 59 seconds. Revised periodically. For information, contact Agape Ministries, Park Avenue Church, 2600 Park Ave., Titusville, FL 32780.

Sheets, Dutch. *Intercessory Prayer: How God Can Use Your Prayers to Move Heaven and Earth*. Ventura, Calif.: Regal Books, 1996.

Sheets, Dutch. *The River of God*. Ventura, Calif.: Regal Books, 1998.

Sherrer, Quin, and Ruthanne Garlock. *Prayers Women Pray: Intimate Moments with God*. Ann Arbor:

Servant Publications, 1998.

Sherrer, Quin, and Ruthanne Garlock. *A Woman's Guide to Getting Through Tough Times.* Ann Arbor: Servant Publications, 1998.

Sherrer, Quin, and Ruthanne Garlock. *A Woman's Guide to Spiritual Warfare.* Ann Arbor: Servant Publications, 1991.

Wagner, Peter. *Your Spiritual Gifts: How to Find Your Gifts and Use Them to Bless Others.* Ventura, Calif.: Regal Books, 1994.

Also by the Authors

By Quin Sherrer

Miracles Happen When You Pray

* * * * *

By Quin Sherrer and Ruthanne Garlock

How to Forgive Your Children
How to Pray for Your Family and Friends
A Woman's Guide to Spiritual Warfare
The Spiritual Warrior's Prayer Guide
A Woman's Guide to Breaking Bondages
A Woman's Guide to Spirit-Filled Living
A Woman's Guide to Getting Through Tough Times
Prayers Women Pray

* * * * *

By Quin Sherrer and Laura Watson

A Christian Woman's Guide to Hospitality

* * * * *

By Ruthanne Garlock

Before We Kill and Eat You
Fire in His Bones
The Christian in Complete Armour, Volumes 1-3
(Senior editor for abridged edition of the
Puritan classic by William Gurnall)

Spend More Time in His Presence

Rivers of Revival
*Neil T. Anderson &
Elmer L. Towns*

With wonderful, God-
given insight, Neil
Anderson and Elmer
Towns show how to
personally experience
revival—and be used
by God to spread it.

Hardcover
ISBN 08307.19342

**Breaking the Bands
of Barrenness**
Frank Damazio

Spiritual despair and
disappointment can
cripple a church.
Here's hope and
encouragement to walk
in the life-producing
promises God has for
His Church.

Hardcover
ISBN 08307.23374

The Rising Revival
*C. Peter Wagner &
Pablo Deiros, Editors*

Massive revival has
been sweeping through
Argentina. Discover
how it all began with
firsthand accounts by
leaders God has used to
bring revival to
Argentina.

Hardcover
ISBN 08307.21398

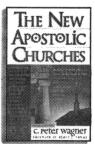

**The New Apostolic
Churches**
C. Peter Wagner

C. Peter Wagner
explains the New
Apostolic Reformation, a
grassroots phenomenon
in which God is raising
up churches and leaders
to help fulfill the Great
Commission.

Hardcover
ISBN 08307.21363

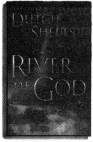

The River of God
Dutch Sheets

Dutch Sheets, author of
the best-selling
Intercessory Prayer,
describes what we must
do to prepare for
revival with biblical
teaching, in the light of
the Holy Spirit's power.

Hardcover
ISBN 08307.20731

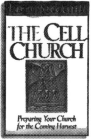

The Cell Church
Larry Stockstill

Throughout the world,
cell-based churches are
evangelizing and disci-
pling millions of new
believers. But can it
work in your city, at
your church? Of course
it can, and Pastor Larry
Stockstill shows you
how in *The Cell Church.*

Hardcover
ISBN 08307.20723

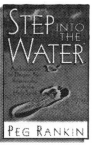

Step into the Water
Peg Rankin

With wisdom and
clarity, best-selling
author Peg Rankin leads
Christians step by step
into the river of God,
where life, vitality and
purpose are found.

Paperback
ISBN 08307.21452

Beyond the Veil
Alice Smith

If you long for a deeper
relationship with your
loving Father, this book
will simply and clearly
light your pathway into
His presence.

Paperback
ISBN 08307.20707

Learn to Fight on Your Knees